To Keep
Moving

Also by Donald Hall:

Poetry

Exiles and Marriages
The Dark Houses
A Roof of Tiger Lilies
The Alligator Bride
The Yellow Room
The Town of Hill
A Blue Wing Tilts at the Edge of the Sea
Kicking the Leaves
The Toy Bone

Prose

String Too Short to be Saved
Henry Moore
Writing Well
Dock Ellis: In the Country of Baseball
Goatfoot Milktongue Twinbird
Remembering Poets: Reminiscences and Opinions

To Keep Moving

Essays 1959-1969
By Donald Hall

HOBART & WILLIAM SMITH
COLLEGES PRESS
in Association with
Seneca Review

Geneva, N.Y. 1980

Library of Congress
Catalog Card No.:   79-90398
          Hall, Donald
                    To Keep Moving, Essays 1959-1969
Geneva, N.Y.: Hobart & William Smith Colleges Press
175 p.
7910   790817

ISBN 0-934888-02-7 (paper)

Hobart & William Smith Colleges Press Books are published by Hobart
& William Smith Colleges, Geneva, N.Y. 14456. *Seneca Review* is
published by Hobart & William Smith Colleges.

Printed in the United States of America.

Acknowledgements

Some of these essays have appeared, in some form or part, in the following books and periodicals: *Michigan Quarterly Review; Walt Whitman, A Choice of His Verse* (Faber); *Contemporary American Poetry* (Penguin Books, Inc.); *The Pleasures of Poetry* (Harper & Row); "Longfellow" (Spoken Arts); *The New York Times Book Review; The Atlantic Monthly; The American Scholar; The Poet as Critic* (Northwestern University Press); *Whittier: A Selection of His Poems* (Laurel Editions, Dell Books); and *Isis* (Holywell Press, Oxford). Every effort has been made to trace the ownership of all copyrighted material in this book and to obtain permission for its use. The editors and author express their grateful acknowledgement to these journals and publishers listed above for permission to reprint here.

for Dorothy Foster

Contents

Introduction: To Keep Moving (1980)   1

Ah, Love, Let Us Be True (1959)   7

A Literature Of Synthesis (1959)   19

Whittier And History (1961)   23

A Note On Longfellow (1966)   38

The Artless Art (1960)   40

Literary Little England (1960)   48

The Uses Of Free Verse (1961)   56

American Poetry Now (1961)   59

Poems Without Legs (1963)   71

Writers In The Universities (1965)   79

An Ethic Of Clarity (1968)   90

Four Kinds Of Reading (1968)   98

Poets On The Platform (1966)   104

Metallic Flowers (1966)   109

The Inward Muse (1965)   115

Whitman: The Invisible World (1967)   132

The Poet And The Battle (1965)   150

Waking Up The Giant (1969)   153

The Expression Without The Song (1969)   160

To Keep
Moving

Introduction: To Keep Moving

1.

IN 1961 I was thirty-three, and had published two books of poems. Editing the Penguin *Contemporary American Poets*, I said in my introduction: "...typically the modern artist...has acted as if restlessness were a conviction, and has destroyed his own past in order to create a future. He has said to himself, like the policeman to the vagrant, 'Keep moving.' " I had in mind artists like Yeats, Picasso, Stravinsky...But, reading literary criticism by poets, one does well to understand that on one level the theories *always* gloss the poets' own views of themselves. Mr. Eliot was concerned with "Hamlet and His Problems," but he spoke from the vantage point of Mr. Eliot's problems. My vagrant-policeman was based, not only on James Joyce or Gertrude Stein, but on someone considerably closer to home.

These essays exemplify a changing, possibly a floundering mind; at any rate, it was a mind that *wanted* to change. In the Penguin introduction, I was trying to sum up the condition of American poetry at the moment — an act of summary I performed every few years. In my senior year at college I had published "Richard Wilbur and Others" in the school magazine. A year later, while I was at Oxford, I wrote an introduction to "American Poets Since the War" for readers of an English monthly; the poets were especially Lowell, Wilbur, and Roethke. Two or three years later, I did a similar piece for *New World Writing*. As I look back over these early surveys, I am astonished by their complacency — by their unquestioning acceptance of literary appearances. Appropriately enough, I set out to defend the new poets against people who thought poetry ended with Frost, or with Eliot, or with Auden, or with Karl Shapiro; but I bragged about how wonderfully America subsidized her poets in the universities; I did not notice the absence of black writers, or the relative absence of women; I indicated no suspicion that poetry might not forever be written in iambics by white, male, associate professors about animals and foreign churches.

2.

The first essay collected here belongs to 1959, and indicates some of the dissatisfaction that I had begun to discover. And things changed quickly, once they started changing. I discovered Robert Creeley, Denise Levertov, Gary Snyder; I discovered free verse! More important for me, in 1957 and 1958 I began to work on poems which made no reasonable sense to me, but which I felt compelled to write; these poems — I think "The Long River" was the first of them — made fantastic images.

Looking over the record as collected in this book, I recognize or remember some sources of change. My first book of poems, *Exiles and Marriages*, appeared in 1955. In 1957 *The New Poets of England and America* was published, an anthology which I co-edited with Robert Pack and Louis Simpson. Thoughtful, rather negative reviews of my poems — especially by Stanley Kunitz in *Poetry* and William Arrowsmith in *Hudson* — struck me with force. And when I read over our anthology after publication, I was depressed at our lack of ambition — especially among the younger of us. But these sources are merely literary; there is always something else. My father died of cancer two weeks after *Exiles and Marriages* was published. He was fifty-two years old, and had spent his latter years planning for retirement. Everywhere I looked in his life, I saw him self-thwarted by his need to follow not his own desires and wishes but the desires and wishes of others, especially his elders. I was twenty-seven years old, and I became aware that I had written my poems for the approval of my elders. Complacency was a way of never questioning anything, of taking what was given, of praising the hand that fed you. With my father's death I felt not only my own mortality, but my complicity in death-in-life. The skill I had struggled for seemed shallow, the poems domestic and self-satisfied, articulate structures of self-limitation. I did not want to drown in shallow waters.

3.

When I left college in 1951 I spent two years at Oxford,

and became aware of national identity by living in another country. Part of this awareness turns up in argument, in two articles from 1960 which embody my quarrel with English friends. Another part is more positive. When I took my first job teaching, in 1957, I moved to the midwest, having lived most of my life in New England. Again, strangeness made for awareness. At the University of Michigan, I taught a small discussion class in American literature, and I taught it many times. I had never studied our literature, and now I began to explore its separate identity. In this book there are essays and notes which grew out of this awareness.

4.

In 1961, I announced "something so new I lack words for it," and a few years later I found some words to describe the poetry of fantasy. I spent a good many years, in my own work, trying to make poems without legs, to achieve expression without song. After several years of working with irrational materials, I began psychotherapy with an analyst in Ann Arbor. Doctrines of psychoanalysis enter late essays here; sometimes psychiatric jargon enters them and harms them. I should say that the jargon came from my reading and not from my doctor. If I spoke to him using phrases like "oral incorporation," his eyebrows would flutter like Viennese butterflies, and he would complain that he did not know what I was talking about.

In Freud I found a materialist theology to explain experiences of the imagination. When I worked on a poem, I would bring it to my doctor, not in manuscript but in summary, and we would discuss it and inquire into it as if it were a dream. My poems became more dream-like. While "The Inward Muse" is touched by my reading in psychoanalysis — and distorted — there are subtler influences operating on an essay like "An Ethic of Clarity," which insists upon the ability of humans to change their lives. Although I had wished earlier "to keep moving," although I had courted literary change, I had found it difficult to hope for true change within myself. I felt subject to something I could not control; I felt like a chip on the stream, although I understood that I was both chip and stream. Now with help I learned a new conviction: "Man is a bird that can change the shape of his beak." Maybe I should arrange to have this sentence carved on my gravestone.

5.

"Man...his..."; the pronouns are male. Reading over these essays, I realize how much I have learned the plural strategy in recent years; in these old essays, "the poet" and "the critic" is "he." I have not revised my pronouns — though twice I have removed from an essay an egregiously sexist analogy — in order to make myself look politically better than I was. For that matter, I have wanted a hundred times to remove some suggestion about poetry which now embarrasses me — but if this collection has any interest, it lies in recording one person's change over time: to alter that record by retrospect would misrepresent the moment. Thus I retain my slurs on the Beat Generation...and so forth.

I have, however, made a few changes: I have added

serial commas; I have omitted repetitions where I found it possible; I have made small changes for style, grammar, and clarity. Here and there, I have argued with myself in a footnote or a postscript. The end of "The Expression Without The Song" is new, not a revision of idea but a substitution of example.

All but one of these pieces has appeared before, in periodical or book. "The Artless Art" is published here for the first time, or largely; I wrote it for an English magazine that commissioned it and found it too harsh. Later, I used the beginning dialogue, with the names turned into pseudonyms, for an introduction to an anthology of English poetry.

For whatever may prove useful here, I have too many people to thank. I hope that they will know who they are.

D.H.
Wilmot, N.H.
15 April 1980

Ah, Love, Let Us Be True (1959)

IN POLITICS, a reform movement cleans out city hall in one election; by the next time the polls are open the racketeers have taken over the reform movement. When Irving Howe wrote "This Age of Conformity," in 1954, he awoke many intellectuals to their casual conservatism; he started with courage in the time of McCarthy slogans that have dwindled, five years later, into clichés of complacency. Now David Brinkley can furrow his brow to ask Robert Frost, in a television interview, if he is not concerned about conformity in America; and John Aldridge publicly searches for heresy by deriving it from the Greek *hairesis*. It is not surprising that reviewers, from the quarterlies to *Time*, should blame the young poets for being married and having children, although fatherhood would seem to be about as conformist as supper. The reviewers are appealing, for the most part, to the ghostly image of *le poetè maudit*; yet it is interesting, if only because it is so contrary to the tenets of the new criticism, that so many of them discuss the social class and behavior of the poets. I suggest that they pick their slogans from the anticonformist air because the poems contain uses of domesticity that disturb them. And I suggest that their disturbance is valid, but that they misunderstand its cause: domesticity is not directly connected with conformity, and domesticity is the real enemy. Conformity is social and public and protective; domesticity for the poet has uses that inhibit his extension as an artist.

The social behavior of the poet is irrelevant to the question of domesticity in his poems. To mention Wallace Stevens at Hartford Accident and Indemnity, or Yeats with his poems to his children, is to win your argument with a critic who demands specific social irregularity in a poet. But if you are a young poet, and you have just won an argument by mentioning Stevens and Yeats, such a victory may seem more like unconditional surrender. We have daughters for whom we write prayers, but we are not Yeats. The anthology of *New Poets of England and America*, which I helped to edit, confronted many of us with our obvious slightness as a generation of poets; we all knew what was *good* about us, but it took a collective annunciation to show us what was bad. None of the reasons I have heard adduced for this slightness (teaching or marriage or the cold war or national prosperity) impresses me. I mean to discriminate symptoms and suggest remedies, but not to speculate on the origins of the disease. I feel that I see a pattern among us of provinciality and evasion, which results in a reliance on the domestic at the expense of the historical. By the historical, I mean the sense of one's own time and the sense of it as a product of the past; this sense requires an act of the imagination by which the past exists in the present, although it is alien. History and contemporary society must be seen together, I think, to be seen at all.

The difference between us and Yeats or Eliot or Pound is not the habits of our daily lives (these poets differed sufficiently among themselves) but one of intelligence, knowledge, and courage. If this is behavior it is behavior of the spirit. It is not the poet's home life that is of literary interest, but any uses to which he may put his home life when he writes poems. If a man writes a love poem to his wife, it is childish to complain that he is conforming to a bourgeois institution; but one might well argue that in a specific poem the poet attaches a relevance to his love, or a value to his affirmation of it, which falsifies his poem and makes it sentimental.

I will need to make (but hardly to prove) a summary statement of my views on the poet's relation to intellectual history. For the past three hundred years, the poet has encountered a number of alternative possibilities for the construction of his *oeuvre*. He begins to write and think in a narrow corner, for he lives in no house or city that is common to the rest of the world, or even to the people of his own nation. No system at hand relates the phenomena he observes, or extends his observation of phenomena. He can stay in the corner and write objectively about what is close to him or subjectively about how his mind deals with his predicament. If he wishes to leave the corner and extend himself, perhaps he can exploit the characteristic dimensions of the church, where theory is made tangible and all events are connected; the difference between the modern religious poet and the religious poet of the sixteenth or early seventeenth century is that the modern makes a gesture of negation to the godless age he lives in; the older poet shares a point of view even with his enemies and discriminates within a general theological agreement about what is universally valid. If the modern poet will not go to church like the later Eliot and Auden, he can perhaps adopt some other systematic arrangement of the world that is not connected with an institution, like Pope with his deism and Pound with his social credit; or perhaps he can invent or amalgamate an amateur religion, like Blake or Wordsworth or Yeats. The virtue of any of these systematic alternatives is that they enlarge the possibilities of subject matter. The spirits who gave Yeats *A Vision* told him that they came to give him metaphors for poetry. They gave him not only metaphors he used in poems, but an inclusive metaphor of human history by which he extended himself into his greatest poems. The alternative I would attack is the one that remains in the corner, is objective, and is concerned with relationship. The poet says with Hollywood, "In this mixed-up world, all we have is each other," or with Matthew Arnold, "Ah, love, let us be true/To one another!"

Now fidelity is not reprehensible, nor is the poetry of love inferior to the poetry of this or that. It is the whole statement that is false, with its implied substitution of love for belief. "Dover Beach" is not a love poem; it is a melancholy reflection on intellectual determinism, and love is invoked as a compensation for the losses that history has forced us to sustain. We are asked to be faithful, "...for the world, which seems/To lie before us like a land of dreams,/...Hath really neither joy..." I hope that there are better reasons for fidelity than disillusion. When Shakespeare entertains unhappy reflections on human suffering, in his courtroom of meditation, the thought of his "dear friend" restores losses and ends sorrows. Yet Shakespeare does not turn to love because of despair: his poem describes an emotional sequence to demonstrate the extent of his love; his poem is about love, finally, and not about suffering. When Yeats catalogues his friends or thinks of his daughter, he makes statements of general validity that do not depend upon the relationship itself, but on the attention paid to particular people; in no poem that I recall does he use a relationship as the evasion of another responsibility. Poets have always encountered and used in their poems love and friendship as they have included all experience; Arnold, however, uses it as an alternative to theology or an idea of history.

"Dover Beach" is an historical poem that includes domesticity as a positive force in a negative universe; like so many Victorian poems, its negation is beautiful and its affirmation repulsive. "Gerontion" is a remarkably similar poem, also melancholy in its determined lack of religious belief, but Eliot is no positive thinker, and deceives himself with no puns on the word "faith." If Gerontion deceives himself at all, as "The Hollow Men" was later to suggest, it is in his comfortable notion that his inaction is a historical necessity. Many contemporary poets write as if they had accepted Arnold's directive but had forgotten Arnold's motives; for history is present in their poems only by the historical oddity of its absence. Domesticity is an alternative to history somewhat in the way that subjectivism is an alternative to theology; a major distinction is that the interior world of subjectivism has produced work of high quality. Subjectivism and theology, in contrasting ways, are abstracted from process. History and domesticity occur in time, and their subjects are subject to change. Yet I would argue that an imaginative vision of history resembles theology more profoundly than either of them resemble their more limited alternatives. They share a desire for total relevance. Really, they seem to represent wholeness to

11

different types of mind: the historical mind is secular, sequential, and conceives in temporal terms; the theological mind conceives of absolutes in spatial, static figures. Of course a major characteristic of contemporary literature has been a mixture, wherein an historical entity is absorbed by a theological sensibility; change has been emphasized by spatial metaphor, as in the copresence of the temporally discrete in Eliot, Pound, and Joyce. In Eliot's poems we can see the secular intellect developing by degrees into an intellect that resembles the poet's consistent imagination.

Subjectivism, which has occupied and displayed most of the best minds in French and English for a century and a half, has undergone no new developments in recent years. Richard Wilbur has moved from *The Beautiful Changes* ("Caught Summer is always an imagined time,") to *Ceremony* ("We milk the cow of the world, and as we do/We whisper in her ear, 'You are not true.' "), to *Things of this World*, the title of which indicates its thematic insistence on the objective. He seems representative of an increasing impatience, among poets, with subjectivism as a contemporary alternative. It seems played out. Andrew Marvell could once say, with his masterful irony, "Meanwhile the mind from pleasure less/Withdraws into its happiness," and tell you of the pleasures while he qualified the morality of his inner retreat. Wordsworth, that capitalist of the imagination, crept into the strong room of recollection to fondle collected emotions, while outside in the new cities of England the world he rejected created poverty and early death to make the rich richer. It was Keats, among the English romantics, who most clearly saw the frailty of romantic subjectivism. However much he admired the urn, however much emotion its beauty inspired, he finally feels only the disparity between the world of permanent imagination and the world of change. He rejects the naive limitations of the urn's philosophy. Yeats sailed through subjectivism and out into something else, for when he reached Byzantium it was to sing "Of what is past, or passing, or to come." When the young poet Yeats announced his departure for Innisfree, it was a departure that would foresee no backward looks. We were asked to dance in the woods with Fergus, and "brood on hopes and fear no more," in the "deep wood's woven shade" of the imagination. The three Chinamen of Yeats' "Lapis Lazuli" climb a mountain that resembles Byzantium, not Innisfree, for when they are high enough,

> On all the tragic scene they stare.
> One asks for mournful melodies;
> Accomplished fingers begin to play.
> Their eyes mid many wrinkles, their eyes,
> Their ancient, glittering eyes, are gay.

It is through tragic art that we comprehend, and even accept, process and change. What the Chinamen see is the human history that Fergus and Wordsworth turn their backs on. History is change, and change is death. Yeats took the final step (possibly the step that makes us impatient with subjectivism) by which the inner world becomes not a fiction useful for escape, but a value by which we judge and interpret the objective world. Yeats makes subjectivism historical. His development is a lesson for anyone. The gifted young author of *The Wanderings of Oisin* was discontented with his gifts; his searches took him into the theater and into a variety of esoteric religions; and think what you will of its spookery, it was *A Vision* that allowed his talents their range, for *A Vision* is a vision of history.

But our problem has not been that of Yeats, and our solution will have to be our own. Instead of inviting ourselves to Innisfree, we have been writing about families and friends, and rejoicing in our limitations. The beat poets, with their frantic peer-group of the "six best poets now writing" and their poems and prefaces addressed to each other, resemble the apparently opposite academic poets with their child- and home-worship. The feeling that is common (not only to the poets but to the whole generation, whether beat or silent — for beatness is only the noise of silence) is the sense that only the local and tangible is safe in a world without meaning; or that only these few friends exist to understand anything in a society of the living dead. Flux and chaos are the terrors outside our circles or our houses, and our images of respite look like statuary.

When Eliot and Pound were our age, they wrote out of a sense of history which no one now seems to possess. They had no systematic theory of history, but they had an imagination of it, and they had sufficient knowledge to begin to discern connections and disconnections. The result was a relevance as universal as a secular intellect allows, for history is the secular totality. They imagined the past in the present. The critical image of the great writers of the world in the same room, which Pound originated in *The Spirit of Romance* and Eliot borrowed for "Tradition and the Individual Talent," depends upon the same imagination that produces a Mr. Appollinax or the social complexity of *Mauberley*. The past is not only a constant judge of the present, but we are reminded both of what endures and what changes. We are joined and separated, and in the experience of separation we acquire the reality of the discrete. It is an extension of the spirit into time.

Copresence must be distinguished from something it superficially resembles, which, since the word is vulgar, I will call "timelessness." The latter is anti-historical and anti-intellectual. It says that history is bunk, that human nature never changes, that poems must include only eternal verities and omit any word that might ever need a footnote. It is a set of attitudes that requires labors neither of mind nor imagination. The truly historical imagination involves the copresence of the alien, not the domestication of the strange into the familiar. The historical man finds it neither just nor comforting to insist that he and Ghengis Khan and G.K. Chesterton and Eric the Red and Horace Gregory are precisely the same. The imagination of copresence precisely makes the alien tangible, but tangibly alien. The middle-class belief that all times and places are equally valuable is a kind of relativism that makes an atheist take side looks at Rome. Domesticity is the specious timelessness of relationships. Domesticity is the evasion of history, for us and for Matthew Arnold — but Arnold at least included history in his poem.

The methods of failure are as numerous as the men who attempt to write poems. There is a way of writing historically, and avoiding both subjectivism and domesticity, which evades poetry as well and which needs particular mention. To write honestly about our society is to be subversive, and yet a poem that is merely subversive can hardly exist. It is not, of course, necessary to see two sides of a one-sided coin ("Does Lynching Have a Silver Lining?"), but a poem that entirely represents the world that it hates, and excludes representation of the world of poetry and the imagination that it loves, ultimately fails and we do not return to it, however accurate its portrait of the society may be. It seems that a poem needs a contrary force, a standard of value against which the poverty of our society is judged; and this can be a force of the imagination alone, a quality of the vision of ugliness, and not a part of the linear structure of the poem. Surely Kenneth Fearing is excellently subversive and yet unreadable because of the frailty of his imagination. The best of E. E. Cummings is subversive (yet on the subject of spring rather than of Cambridge ladies, Cummings sounds like Norman Vincent Peale) and eventually reveals its poverty. Some contemporary poets, fearing the dangers of mere subversion, will bring in the domestic as an affirmative stopgap, the way Fearing will mention blue sky or Cummings flowers. If you wish to include the life of your own times in poems, you must avoid both barren subversion and phony affirmation. For this reason, few young poets write about their times now, but go to Greek myths or Biblical stories. They are not using history, to which our entrance is always from our own time, but our small store of common knowledge. There is nothing really wrong with these sources, of course, if you do not go to them for the safety of their "timeless" authority, but few of the "Adam and Eve"'s or "Herakles: a Quadruple Sestina"'s of recent years justify themselves by their obvious excellence.

To try to see in what direction we might move, perhaps we can look at our writers of the immediate past. The American intellectual has generally been an eclectic, a pillager of castles like William Randolph Hearst. It is not so necessary for a European to know things; he breathes the past in his own air. The American must acquire the air of thirty centuries, not forgetting his own. What we sometimes dismiss as pedantry in Pound and Eliot — the languages, the historical references, the quotations — is the ground of their greatness. The young poets in America have failed in knowledge; we lack languages and we lack familiarity with other cultures and other disciplines. Most of us remain entirely ignorant of the intellectual life of our century and know nothing of economics, physics, psychology or even the modern science of linguistics. Of course good poets, not only Eliot but later Americans like Yvor Winters and Allen Tate, have rejected the ideas of their age as well as their societies, but their rejections have been made consciously, after acquaintance, and not accidentally, out of ignorance. We are a provincial generation, largely unaware of the past, of our own tradition, or of the nature of our limitations. Most of us have sheltered in the protection of the intimate.

If we are to change, we will not change only because we want to; yet a sense of failure is the only possible basis for change. I talk as if such a change were intellectual and volitional, yet it is a change of character in the poet; he must see the new life. The voices will have to speak to us before we can find the metaphors for poetry; but the poems that a greater historical vision can bring to us are poems of a greater complexity. The evasion of history by domesticity is a fault both moral and technical, for the quality of a poem resides not only in the degree of its coherence but in the quantity of units that cohere. History is necessarily more complex than domesticity because it includes it. Thus a possible avenue of extension for a domestic poet would lie not in rejecting his subject matter, but in adding to it a judgment of it based upon an act of the historical imagination.*

---

*1980: I have ended the essay at its next-to-last paragraph. In the final paragraph which I omit, I felt obliged to list some poets I admired, and to whom I now seem condescending.

A Literature Of Synthesis (1959)

WHEN Henry James wrote his *Hawthorne*, for the *English Men of Letters* series, he listed thirty-three "items of high civilization" which were absent from the American scene: "No State...No sovereign, no court,...no palaces, no castles, nor manors, nor old country-houses, nor parsonages, nor thatched cottages nor ivied ruins;... — no Epsom nor Ascot!" As ever, James sounds like an American. One never hears a European complain that the United States lacks thatched cottages. James' list resembles an inventory sheet from the estate of a William Randolph Hearst: "Items of High Civilization; Item, One castle; Item, One old country-house..."

Charges against James that he forsook his nationality concern his biography, not the spirit of his fiction. The literary nationalist would limit a writer's subject matter to the local, and the effect of this limitation will vary according to the locality. To deal with Des Moines only is to be anti-historical, which is to say anti-intellectual, for Des Moines has a shallow past; it's like a shallow dish, and can hold little food. To ignore antiquity is to limit drastically your understanding of the present. The American writer must write about Des Moines in a context which is historical. But if you are Thomas Hardy, you may deal with Wessex only, for Wessex includes the Roman Empire and the Middle Ages. Provincialism is compatible with great literature in a country with a long history.

The best American literature has tended to be cosmopolitan, and in this characteristic it differs markedly from English literature, which is insular. The English in Italy simply transported England to a better climate. Part of the strength of their literature is its very insularity, with its eternal subject of the English class system. But when an American writer attempts to be 100 percent American, it is proper to be wary. He may write one good book out of local feeling, and then find he can write no more. Or he may settle for superficiality, like most writers. If he is lucky, he may succeed by imposing a cosmopolitan symbolism on his local material, like Faulkner at his best.

Henry James is the first American author to develop. He is the first to produce that quantity of distinguished work which can be called an *oeuvre*. Reading through his work, we are aware of a refinement of literary technique which we must recognize as the self-education of a master. T. S. Eliot is another member of the small congregation of American writers who have learned to improve their art after their first successes. It is customary to look at these men as renegades who fled their country because it lacked literary culture; some critics have even attributed their departure to petulance over a lack of appreciation. It makes more sense to see them acting out, in their migrations, the eclecticism which they needed to acquire in order not to survive but to grow.

It is a matter of material. You make poems and stories

out of yourself, but the self is no *tabula rasa*. It is acquired through experience, and both the quality and the quantity of the experience matter to the writer. America is by nature an aggregate, a glorious hodge-podge of foreign tongues and customs, but no amount of chatter about Indians can push the landing of the pilgrims back before 1620.* We have horizontal variety of experience, but we lack history's vertical experience. We have energy, but we lack depth. Energy makes for a start, and depth makes for endurance. It is American energy which makes possible our cosmopolitan search for the past.

I am saying that what is American about Henry James and Eliot necessitated that they leave America. Born in a country without a past, they travelled like tourists in the gift shop of the world, and picked up what they could use for material: a piece of classical marble here, a phrase of Sanskrit there. James wrote out of a "sense of the past" that his Newmans and Newsomes do not share. Much of the endeavor of his art is to understand, and to acquire for fiction, this alien and urgent sense. He is utterly unlike the Europeans among whom he chose to live. For the literate European James' gift shop is the air they breathe.

American literature is the literature of synthesis. For an American writer, to use the foreign is not to lose nationality, which is as difficult to lose as your fingerprints, but precisely to be American. Today it is no longer so necessary to act out our eclecticism by living abroad, though almost all our writers still spend some of their youth outside the United States. So many Hearsts,

---

*1980: And no amount of research into Native American religion can change an Anglo into an Iroquois.

21

millionaires and poets both, have filled so many warehouses, both museums and *Waste Lands*, with so many *objects*, that our country is a storehouse of the past of the world. Our tradition has become an ambitious one: to include all traditions.

Whittier And History (1961)*

I

NO ONE is less fashionable than John Greenleaf Whittier. I suspect that it is more acceptable to admire Alfred Austin. The Quaker's reputation has suffered heavily for its long white whiskers, and his lines:

> *Why should the unborn critic whet*
> *For me his scalping-knife?*

have become an idle boast. The born critic has not read John Greenleaf Whittier since the eighth grade, where he spent an art period sketching the farm in *Snow-Bound,* or acted Stonewall Jackson in a dramatic tableau of "Barbara Frietchie." This ignorance is the critic's loss. What Whittier represents of our past makes him an American figure

---

*1980: This essay introduced a selection of Whittier's poems published by Laurel Editions of Dell Books in 1962.

of particular historical interest, not so much for poetry as for politics, but his poetical talents are considerable. Although he is not a great poet, he is often a good one.

His reputation has paid the price which is exacted of extreme popularity. Whittier was widely hated in his young manhood because of his radical politics, but when *Snow-Bound* was published at the end of the Civil War his abolitionism had become the law of the land, and it was possible for him to have a public success. When he died in 1892, towns and colleges had been named for him, Harvard had given him two honorary degrees and made him an Overseer, Matthew Arnold had visited him, and, it had been reported, a volume of his poems had been seen on Tennyson's table. He lived to see his birthday celebrated in schools like the birthday of George Washington. Only Oliver Wendell Holmes survived him among "the New England poets," and not even Longfellow was so widely loved.

It was a glorious conclusion to the life which had started on a poor farm in East Haverhill, Massachusetts, in 1807. Whittier was born on the land which an ancestor had settled in the seventeenth century, and which Whittiers had farmed ever since. He describes the Quaker farmhouse and the simple life in *Snow-Bound*. Whittier was largely self-taught, for there was little help coming from the local school. Years later, introducing an appendix of early poems, he excused them as "the weak beginnings of the graduate of a small country district school, sixty years ago." One schoolteacher, however, performed the service of a catalyst by introducing him to the poems of Burns when he was fourteen. It was Burns whose poetic example Whittier chose to follow. Later he wrote about reading these poems aloud:

Bees hummed, birds twittered, overhead
    I heard the squirrels leaping,
The good dog listened while I read,
    And wagged his tail in keeping.

The significance of Whittier's attachment to Burns has usually been overlooked.

Whittier is that rare creature, a peasant poet — though the phrase rankles on the American ear. Lowell, Longfellow, and Holmes were patricians; Longfellow studied at Bowdoin with Nathaniel Hawthorne and Franklin Pierce; Holmes and Lowell went to Harvard, and all three were professors there. Whittier, on the other hand, grew up at hard labor on a farm which did not encourage the pursuit of letters. The height of his schooling was his brief attendance at the Haverhill Academy, where he paid part of his tuition by making ladies' slippers.

The first editor to print Whittier's verse was William Lloyd Garrison, then young and little known. These two great abolitionists met, not in the cause, but as editor and poet. Only slightly older, Garrison was greatly impressed by Whittier's early verse, and drove out to the farm in his carriage to call on the farmer-poet. When he tried to convince Whittier's father of his son's talent, in order to urge that more education would be useful, the old man answered, "Sir, poetry will not give him *bread.*" But Whittier — author of:

And must I always swing the flail,
And help to fill the milking pail?
I wish to go away to school;
I do not wish to be a fool.

—was enabled, long after school was over, to give his father the lie. In time, "...homes of wealth...gladly welcomed e'en a rustic boy." As with other peasant poets, poetry allowed him to leave the farm.

Besides Burns, he admired low-church Cowper, and Byron for his politics, and Milton for his politics and morals. He liked the corn-law poems of Ebenezer Elliott, who was "to the artisans of England what Burns was to the peasantry of Scotland." He liked Gray's "Elegy," and predictably disliked Whitman and dismissed Shelley as lacking virtue. Often his praise of a writer was in terms of his politics.

As a Quaker, Whittier was bound to hate slavery; Quakers were among the first abolitionists everywhere. Also as a good Quaker, who wore Quaker dress and thee'd and thou'd most of his life, he was bound to oppose violence. Yet Whittier was happy to use any political means short of bodily harm, including political opportunism, to further the ends of abolition. He and Garrison quarreled on this question, for Garrison believed in sheer moral force uncontaminated by party. Whittier's middle years were devoted to the fight against slavery, and most of his poems for twenty-five years were created for the struggle. It is a pity that few of his abolitionist poems are readable today; as he wrote, "Such as they are, they belong to the history of the Anti-Slavery movement..."

Correctly and without false modesty, he wrote:

> O Freedom! if to me belong
> Nor mighty Milton's gift divine,
>   Nor Marvell's wit and graceful song,
>   Still with a love as deep and strong
> As theirs, I lay, like them, my best gifts on thy shrine.

If we have the sense that Whittier's poems are never quite up to Whittier, he has given us the explanation which he wanted to believe himself. Words like freedom and tyranny were incredibly strong to Whittier, and to others of his time. Used to sell soap or a political party, these words are cheapened for us. Whittier would have said that the small town in rural New England, run by town meeting, was the truest democracy America ever had. It was more democratic than Athens because it was a society of free men.

Whittier represented a survival of this democracy. Boston and Harvard, in the decades before the Civil War, showed themselves as generous toward escaped slaves as they were later toward Sacco and Vanzetti. Abolitionists were requested not to rock the boat, and the boat consisted of sound investments in the products of southern cotton. On State Street, Boston's version of Wall, money made morals. Here are some lines of Whittier on the portrait of a man who sold his allegiance:

A moony breadth of virgin face,
  By thought unviolated;

* * * * * * * *

How keen to scent the hidden plot!
  How prompt wert thou to balk it,
With patriot zeal and peddler thrift,
  For country and for pocket.

The early days of abolition were difficult. Whittier knew "the fierce mob's hounding down," on several occasions, at a time when men were murdered for holding his views.

A man died in Washington, as a result of imprisonment, whose crime was to distribute a pamphlet by Whittier.

The cities were corrupt; even the Quakers in Philadelphia were unwilling to offend their southern customers. It was seventeenth-century, rural democracy that Whittier reflected. He was born between the Revolution and the War of 1812 when America, late a colony, believed herself *against* repression and foreign masters and *for* liberty and self-determination. The Monroe Doctrine, the Mexican War, the Spanish-American War and two World Wars have made the old talk about liberty an anachronism, as Whittier felt the treatment of slaves and Indians had long made it an hypocrisy.

Whittier worked intermittently as an editor of several newspapers, but his major means of support was his writing. In 1836, he sold the farm and moved to Amesbury, to the house where he lived until his death. In the years after *Snow-Bound* and its successor *The Tent on the Beach* had made his fame, he lived in a celebrated retirement. Many young people befriended him, including Sarah Orne Jewett, and his correspondence was extensive. Toward the end of his long life it was his sad duty to write many an elegy for old friends and associates. In the course of one, he defined his necessity:

> *I take, with awe, the task assigned;*
> *It may be that my friend might miss,*
> *In his new sphere of heart and mind,*
> *Some token from my hand in this.*

It remained for Oliver Wendell Holmes to write the elegy for Whittier on his death in September, 1892.

II

"I am a *man*, and not a mere verse-writer," the poet said, yet here we owe the reader an account of his poetical qualities. It is easy to disparage Whittier. The attitude which derides his simplicity — or what he called, "The dear delight of doing good" — in favor of the poetry of evil, is the Calvinism of twentieth-century atheists, a religion which prevails in the universities. Parochial cynicism misses the point that Whittier's goodness is true and representative, and also that he most clearly recognizes evil.

However, Whittier wrote too much — dedications, birthday poems, elegies, thanks for gifts, memorials, epitaphs, responses to public events — and much of it is poor. One finds in the poems repetitive movements of thought, particularly one in which a complexity is evoked and then evaded by recourse to a predictable rhyme with "heaven," or "Lord"; religion is used as a third-act curtain. A few metaphors, like "homespun breasts," are remarkably absurd, and in some cases whole poems can be added to the list of the ridiculous; "The Cable Hymn" is one of the great series of nineteenth-century odes to modern inventions; Whittier uses, among other kennings, "mystic cord" and "magic thread," and he predicts that the invention will bring about universal peace. But these are faults which do not detract from his achievements.

Our age should have many a surprise in reading Whittier. It may be odd to discover the influence of later Yeats:

And daft McGregor on his raids
In Costa Rica's everglades,

in *Snow-Bound*, but there it is; and here is an imperfect anticipation of Auden:

> *A green-haired woman, peony-cheeked, beneath*
> *Impossible willows. . . .*

More defensibly, there is the presence of synesthesia, surprising in a rustic poet: "The hymn of sunset's painted skies." There is a kind of strong, broad wit visible in the lines on the portrait of the sell-out, or in:

> *Saving, as shrewd economists, their souls*
> *And winter pork with the least possible outlay*
> *Of salt and sanctity. . . .*

Whittier is not the cozy bard of winter evenings on the farm in these lines, nor is he the patriarch who appears in the Famous Americans series of postage stamps. He is the lean young man with violent eyes revealed in an early portrait.

Whittier's imagination is most intense when it deals with the miraculous. Often this can be seen in the verbal texture alone, and it can be startlingly good:

> *Sudden our pathway turned from night;*
> *The hills swung open to the light;*

But it is not surprising that many of his best poems are legends of the supernatural. Some of his best prose work, too, was accounts of superstition in New England.

But first of all, his images convince the eye:

You catch a glimpse, through birch and pine,
  Of gable, roof, and porch,
The tavern with its swinging sign,
  The sharp horn of the church.

The last line has a novelty of vision which one does not associate with the New England poets. It shocks, and it shocks accurately. More than that, I think that superstition enters again distantly, for it is the church's adversary whom we generally associate with horns.

Metrically, Whittier went to school to Burns. He knew his trade, within his limits, exceedingly well, and he was an inveterate reviser in proof. His limitations included the fact that he never mastered the pentameter line; his best verse is in tetrameter and trimeter. Within the short line, he is fond of metrical inversion, and uses it often to great effect in conjunction with an image that gives pause, like "The sharp horn of the church." Within stanzas, it seems clear that he handled the quatrain more skillfully than any other kind of arrangement. Though some of his good work is in couplets, this form tended to allow his natural verbosity too much license. The longer unit of the quatrain was a true unit, while the couplets were bricks to be piled on top of each other.

He is known more for nostalgia — in *Snow-Bound,* "The Barefoot Boy," and many other poems — than for his wit or his concern with the supernatural, and of course it is true that much of his finest work arises from this emotion. One must remember that nostalgia is *the* great American subject. In one poem he invokes, instead of the Muse, the "Angel of the backward look." As he wrote, most memorably:

31

The hills are dearest which our childish feet
Have climbed the earliest; and the streams most sweet
Are ever those at which our dumb lips drank,
Stooped to their waters o'er the grassy bank.

* * * * * * * *

And still, with inward eye, the traveller sees
In close, dark, stranger streets his native trees.

The parallels in American literature are endless. The wilderness of Natty Bumpo, Huck Finn's boyhood, the vigorous antiquity in Hawthorne, the "too late" of Henry James, F. Scott Fitzgerald's vision of the past, Hemingway's Nick Adams in Upper Michigan, and Faulkner's relicts of the old South all utter the same keen.

Whittier was witness to a social process which probably contributed to his individual nostalgia, a process strangely parallel to the defeat of the South. Rural New England collapsed and died during his lifetime. He sold the old Whittier farm himself; countless others left their small farms to move west or work in the "dark Satanic mills" of Lowell, Lawrence — and ultimately Haverhill. Whittier wrote from these losses, and speaking in the first line of a mill neither dark nor satanic, but a grist mill that has disappeared as everything will disappear.

The timbers of that mill have fed
  Long since a farmer's fires;
His doorsteps are the stones that ground
  The harvest of his sires.

Yet Whittier differs from the parade of nostalgic American writers in one enormous respect; he is somehow optimistic. He recalls his childhood with pleasure, and not at all to contrast innocence and experience. He asks the farmers to return:

> With skill that spares your toiling hands,
>   And chemic aid that science brings,
> Reclaim the waste and outworn lands,
>   And reign thereon as kings!

Come back and I'll give you a tractor.

It is easier to sneer (every tenth-rate mind knows enough to ridicule the idea of progress today) than to understand. There is a paradox, or what seems to the modern mind a paradox, in the combinations which occur in Whittier's mind. For instance, he certainly thinks of slavery as evil; he doesn't attempt to positive-think about it; he is forthright in his denunciation of it and of the institutions which foster it:

> The Church, beneath her trembling dome,
>   Essayed in vain her ghostly charm:
> Wealth shook within his gilded home
>   With strange alarm.

Yet Whittier adds later in this poem:

> But life shall on and upward go;
>   Th'eternal step of Progress beats
> To that great anthem, calm and slow,
>   Which God repeats.

33

He believes in the triumph of goodness the way a Marxist believes in the inexorable movement of history. Yet many Marxists manage to hate the ruling class, although its oppression is economically determined. So Whittier attacked with passion the institutions which he believed were bound to fail. He attacked what did not measure up to the ideal he served. He was tough *because* he had such an ideal of goodness. Again, he represents the old ideal of democracy, which depends upon goodness; the South had never believed in it, and the cities of the mercantile North had discovered that it was an impediment to trade.

Although Whittier can say,

Life is indeed no holiday; therein
Are want, and woe, and sin.

it is obvious that, if by some mistake goodness does not profit on earth, it will be rewarded in heaven. Whittier so desperately insists on the goodness of God that we are reminded that for him it was not simply a churchly axiom; it is an answer to Calvinism, that religion which, as a Quaker, he had excellent reason to despise. A little poem called "The Minister's Daughter" narrates the change of a minister from Calvinism to a belief in the goodness of God. One quatrain particularly presents the contrast:

No more as the cloudy terror
Of Sinai's mount of law,
But as Christ in the Syrian lilies
The vision of God he saw.

It was Whittier who wrote the hymn which begins, "Dear Lord and Father of mankind,/Forgive our foolish ways!"

The Father is stern and good, implacable toward sin and forgiving to the sinner — like a good Quaker.

III

In a further apology for his early poems, Whittier wrote, "That they met with some degree of favor at that time may be accounted for by the fact that the makers of verse were then few in number, with little competition in their unprofitable vocation, and that the standard of criticism was not discouragingly high." It is a pity that standards never rose very high at all, for Whittier could have profited from a climate less generous to its poets. He responded to criticism well, but he was not subjected to it sufficiently, and never developed enough sense of art. Hawthorne wrote that, "Strictly speaking, Whittier did not care much for literature," but Hawthorne died before some of the best work was published. Mostly, Whittier was unaware of literature.

Winfield Townley Scott, author of the one good modern essay on Whittier, has written a poem called "Mr. Whittier," in which he says:

> . . . . *it was important*
> *To stand suddenly struck with the wonder of old*
> *legends in a young land,*
> *To look up at last and see poetry driving a buckboard*
> *around the bend,*
> *And poetry all the time in the jays screeching at the cats*
> *in the dooryard,*
> *Climbing with the thrush into the August noon out of*
> *the boy's sight*

> *As he dawdled barefoot through poetry among the*
> *welts of the goldenrod . . . .*

It is necessary to remember that when Whittier began to write, American literature did not exist, and American material was largely unexploited. Scott goes on about Whittier's peculiar qualities:

> *Carl Schurz, finding him rained in by the stove at the*
> *village store,*
> *Thought "So superior to those about him, and yet so*
> *like them"; and*
> *His official biographer decided that Mr. Whittier's*
> *poetry was the kind*
> *"Written first of all for the neighbors. . . ."*

The quality of the neighbors affected the quality of the poems. Van Wyck Brooks wrote in 1915, in *America's Coming of Age*, "It could really have been said of us then, as it cannot now be said at all, that as a folk we had won a certain coherence, a certain sort of ripeness in the better part of ourselves, which was reflected in the coherence of our men of letters. Whittier, for example, was a common basis, and a very sweet and elevating basis, for a national programme of emotions the like of which no poet since his time has been able to compass."

We might add that it is unthinkable, in 1961, that the words "sweet" or "elevating" could be applied to literature except ironically. The goodness of Whittier is tied to the deeply egalitarian, anti-tyrannical agrarianism of the small towns of New England. Industrialism, trade and communications have conspired to destroy all traces of this society. Neither America nor American poetry has followed the way of thought that Whittier represented The great poet who began writing toward the end of Whittier's life (and whom Whittier could have understood, though he would not have liked him, as he could never have understood T. S. Eliot) was E. A. Robinson, and Robinson was convinced that life was pretty much a bad thing. To me as to most moderns, Robinson's view is more convincing than Whittier's, but this is to be expected, for Robinson's negativism is the weather of our time. To read Whittier requires an effort of the historical imagination; we must learn to cope with goodness and optimism.

Times have changed! The tent of the book-title was pitched on Hampton Beach, which has become a row of ugly cottages, hot dog stands, bars, roller skating rinks, and beer halls. It is hard to see the ocean for the waxed paper. The industries of New England are going the way of the farms, but they leave behind them not cellar holes but slums. The farmers are not returning with "chemic skill," but their great-grandsons drive back in their De Sotos to buy tinted postcards of Franconia Notch.*

---

*1980: And Whittier, California, became famous as the birthplace of a President...

A Note On Longfellow (1966)*

ENRY Wadsworth Longfellow occupies a special position in American literature. He was universally popular in the nineteenth century, not only in the United States but in England. When Queen Victoria received him in 1868, she wrote in her diary that she "noticed an unusual interest among the attendants and servants... When he took leave, they concealed themselves in places from which they could get a good look at him as he passed." His fame was the product of a carefully cultivated career. One might call him the first of a long series of American poets as professional literary men. From college he had written his father, "I most eagerly aspire after future eminence in literature." He graduated at eighteen, furthered his education in Europe, and became a professor at twenty-two. By the time he was forty-seven he was able to retire from his teaching at Harvard and devote himself entirely to the writing of poetry.

*Written for the jacket of a record issued by *Spoken Arts*, printed here to follow "Whittier and History."

He lived in a splendid house on Brattle Street in Cambridge, Massachusetts, and in his elegant study wrote a massive Collected Works.

A large portion of his work is Longfellow's contribution to a myth of the country and the continent. The romantic story of *Evangeline* is an attempt to add color and texture to a part of the world that has felt the lack of a history. Longfellow's sense of history was acute. He came from a New England that tended to turn its face toward the Old, and some of his best writing happened when he saw the old world in the new. Perhaps his best lyric is his "The Jewish Cemetery at Newport," with its "But ah! what once has been shall be no more!" One stanza of that poem, with its wit, intelligence, and brilliant use of poetic rhythm, shows Longfellow at his very best:

> *And thus forever with reverted look*
> *The mystic volume of the world they read,*
> *Spelling it backward, like a Hebrew book,*
> *Till life became a Legend of the Dead.*

The literary reference, to the Book of the Dead, is typical of Longfellow, and so is the delicate nostalgia, the sweet aroma of regret.

The Artless Art (1960)*

THE scene is the office of a magazine in London, where the protagonist, who is an American poet, is calling on an English acquaintance who has become an editor. The editor is a young, intelligent Oxford man who likes novels very much.

Protagonist: You don't seem to review poetry very much in your magazine. In fact you don't seem to *print* poetry very much.

Editor: Oh, it's hard to fit it in. The people here don't care for literature.

Protagonist: Can't you wedge open a little more space for poems, at least? Not mine, of course! Somebody's.

Editor: I suppose we print enough, really. Not much is going on over here, do you think? Things are better in your country, I suppose. I print a lot of poems I don't like.

Protagonist: I think there are some good poeple writing. Of course the magazines are full of ghastly poems by D.J. Enright and people like that, but there are others.

---

*1980: This article was intended for an English audience.

Editor: Oh. I think Dennis is one of the best, really. *A competent dramatist might end his scene here, and let the silence swell with implication, but really the Editor continues:* He isn't pretentious. I like his irony and his tone.

Protagonist: (too shocked to make points) But — he can't write! He doesn't know what a metaphor is! He has no sense of the art! He starts out with one metre and abandons it as soon as it gets difficult! He writes pointless little anecdotes about his travels, full of phoney compassion! He says he's guilty because he's an Englishman and everybody else is a native!

Editor: (cool) Do you think so? Perhaps you're right. I don't suppose Dennis takes his peoms very seriously, actually.

Drama escapes us. Curtain. The protagonist emerges dressed as an essay, and provides a moment of transition by remarking that is is strange but true that most poets, most of the time, seem to have taken poetry seriously; in fact, when he starts to number the good poets who have not taken poetry seriously, he can't get started. Then he implies that the editor thinks that "not much is going on" because he prefers bad poems to good ones. Good poems, the protagonist says, are often ambitious ("pretentious") and they are not always ironical. Sometimes they are solemn and sometimes they are jolly. They are always well written.

* * * * * * * *

Tolerance for incompetent verse has increased, and in exact ratio the tolerant critics have announced that poetry is dead. (Edmund Wilson's essay on the decline of poetry

41

should be read together with his tribute to the verse of Edna St. Vincent Millay.) Tolerance for the incompetent is greater in England than in America (which has its *own* problems). Most poetry in England seems motivated by the notion that words printed in lines are somehow more spiritual than words printed in paragraphs. So we find lines like these:

Standardised dustbins
Fit precisely into the mouth of a large cylinder
Slung on a six-wheeled chassis.

from the latest (some say it's the fourth, some say the eleventh) volume by D. J. Enright. In a literary society with standards of artistry, no poet would publish such lines; or he would publish them only to universal and immediate ridicule.

Incompetence, be it emphasized, is no friend of generations. English poetry has been afflicted by a lack of artistic standards since the time of the experimenters. The sewage of the thirties and the garbage of the forties are only different in flavor from the vomit of the fifties. It is impossible, and pointless, to prove the causes — but perhaps the destruction of bad, old-fashioned literary standards was not followed by a good revolutionary government. Mr. Eliot never criticized younger poets, and the best critic of the thirties, brilliant on his seniors, showed himself incapable of judging anything new. W. H. Auden's affectation of carelessness was followed too literally; Dylan Thomas was looked on as the Messiah of a new religion, rather than as an idiosyncratic rhetorician; and William Empson, who had painfully obvious difficulties with rhyme and metre, became tutor to a generation.

But decades and generations are only invented by critics who want to avoid the serious consideration of literature. The situation of poetry — the sort of thing represented by the Editor — is at least a *little* serious. The good poets of England live out their days in a literary society which has no understanding of the art of poetry. Young men in school may be taught, for all I know, that Empson is a technical master, and if they read the poems in the magazines they will learn that anything goes. They are liable to be worse, as a group, than their elders, since they are nurtured on worse. Free verse works, for instance, when it derives from strong regular metres.* When a second generation writes free verse out of free verse, the rhythm is fainter, less compelling. And the copy of a copy is poorer still. Only a general return to the great models of poetic art — not for imitation of the surface but for recognition of the artistic essence — can ameliorate England's poetic situation.

When the initial form of a short poem is abandoned in its course, the result is a sense of expediency. (Some poets believe in expressive form, and will write a short line if it describes a dwarf, or mix a metaphor to emphasize the theme of miscegenation — but even if errors are deliberate, the effect on the reader is disaster.) Real *vers libre* is a form too, and can be abandoned as wantonly as a metrical pattern or a rhyme scheme. Random asymmetries are capitulations of the sound (or the form in general) to the sense. If William Plomer writes a thirty line tetrameter

---

*1980: I no longer agree with this proposition, which I took from Eliot, and which I repeat later in a note on free verse. Many new poets have written good free verse, who could not tell meter from potatoes.

43

poem which includes two trimeters, one pentameter, and one hexameter — and which rhymes ababa except for stanza three, which is rhymed axaxa — we can only think that he has been unequal to the rigors of the form he chose. The spectacle of his defeat does not encourage us to listen to what he is saying. The correlative error is padding and forcing. When Enright writes a stanza:

And then he gave up to wondering.
For he felt his nails sink into the earth:
Not a moment to lose, he was scrabbling
Dog-like, towards some great hidden worth.

we groan through the last line, "some" ugh ugh "great" ugh ugh — until we come to the cliché rhyme word, which is among other things inappropriate diction. Empson's praised "Missing Dates" forces the rhyme consistently. Another poem in which the sense has defeated the form is:

Thirty days hath September,
April June, and November.
All the rest have thirty-one
Except February, which has twenty-eight

Now this quatrain has seemed enormously funny to me, like the limerick about the young man from Japan*, since

---

*There was a young man from Japan
Whose poems would never scan.
    When he was asked why
    He would reply,
"Well, I simply try to get as many syllables into the last line as I possibly can."

I began to hear poetry sometime in adolescence. But I don't expect it seems funny to the *Times Literary Supplement*. When Hilary Corke recently attacked expedient asymmetries of metre, the *Times* countered with an editorial magnificently titled, "The Muse in Chains." The day has come when the controls of art have come to seem totalitarian!

Yet art is control.

That's not all a *poem* is, but art is what controls the poem, and without control there is no statement. Of course rhythm is not the only means of control. English poets have been even more remarkable in their ignorance of metaphor. One must assume that a man like John Press — who begins the title poem of his last book, "The tongues of fire...lick..." — is not even aware that his clichés *are* metaphors. When Ronald Duncan writes about "your image impaled upon my face," he requires a nose as sharp as a stiletto; really, he simply does not visualize his metaphor. When Roy Fuller writes, "The worker columns *ebb* across the bridge," he puts the water *over* the bridge, instead of under it, and when Graham Hough says that Daphne "*froze* into a laurel tree" he turns two upright solids into a potentially upright liquid. One can quibble, legalistically, about all of these metaphors; but the necessity to quibble shows the inadequacy of the imagination.

Cliché rhymes (earth/birth/worth; death/breath; womb/tomb/ talk/walk/ fire/desire) grow like weeds in every collection, and are only outnumbered by the clichés which are not rhymed. Enright, in his latest book, contributes "tear-stained," "time-honoured," "vast projects" — and numerous paraphrases of common phrases: "Those whom power has not yet tended to corrupt," "Was I born yesterday?," "A fearful symmetry is won." Such allusions are sometimes useful in a poem; when a poet abounds in them, he is artless.

* * * * * * *

Editor: You needn't go on, you know. The point is that you don't care what a poem says. You prefer art to life. Some of us might not agree with you. We might consider you immature.

Protagonist: "Life against art" has never really seemed a serious question to me, because I always thought that art was about life, and that life included art.

Editor: I mean ordinary life, the life that people live.

Protagonist: I don't think that art need be about People Like Us. The nursery, the office, and the consciences of professors and librarians are not the only subjects for literature. Yes, if life means "the life I lead in August 1960," I do think art is more important than it. But only because I think Life is more important than it too.

* * * * * * *

When I talk about the art of poetry, I'm talking about the skill which makes a perfect surface, *through* which we understand the true relevance of the poem. I think that the technique of poetry is serious *because* it tells us about life. The paradox is that only when the world of art exists independently of meaning — unbroken by the importunities of ideas — can the poem begin to exist. Only from an autonomous kingdom of art can the poem tell the truth.

Yeats was always writing parables about this. He sailed out of the natural world to Byzantium in order to look

back and write about the changes of time. His Chinamen
climbed above the chaos of the world, on a piece of lapis
lazuli, in order to understand it in terms of tragic art, their
"mournful melodies." Artists *who fail in their art* are
those who, "break up their lines to weep." Many a poet
who cannot write good poems argues that poems are no
good. People always have a good reason for making
senseless dichotomies, for preferring food and despising
dinner.

Literary Little England (1960)*

L AST winter, in the Essex village where I have been
spending a year, I met a young woman whom a
friend had described as "jolly keen on horses." She was
blonde and handsome and reminded me of Strindberg's
Miss Julie. She was being friendly, and asked me what I
did; I told her that I wrote poems. For a moment I watched
her strong blue eyes waver and water. (In America, too, I
have made this answer; it's a marvelous index of status:
it's as if you said, "Oh, I sell underwear. And do a bit of
kidnapping on the side.") Then she recovered and asked,
"Uh...what sort? The *straight-forward* kind?"

I couldn't, in good conscience, give her the assurance
she wanted. Probably I was forgiven as an American who
couldn't be expected to know the rules of good conduct,
for the English are more tolerant of us than they are of
each other. But the point is that she thought of poetry,
straight-forward or the other kind, as an activity that involved good or bad form — and she was not interested in

---

*1980: This essay was written for Americans.

48

literary technique. To write difficult poetry, in her eyes, was to be precious, and was not to be a decent sort at all. Of course the philistine, if I may dust off that quaint label, is hardly new to the island of Britain. It is only strange to find — as I return to England after six years, and read the good weeklies and monthlies — that the best of the young critics and poets uphold ideas of contemporary verse which can be shared by the horsewoman in Essex. As the poet Robert Conquest says, you cannot laugh it off that Philip Larkin appears to prefer John Betjeman to Ezra Pound. And you cannot laugh it off that Conquest cites this opinion as an appeal to authority.

When I was in England last, studying at Oxford from 1951 to 1953, the old distinctions held true. The young men of the Critical Society met to discuss the later poems of Yeats, while the Poetry Society drew hundreds to listen to Dylan Thomas. On the other hand most of the University stayed in digs and read Hansard or P. G. Wodehouse or nothing at all. And I met a don who had tutored W. H. Auden and who remembered the experience with distaste: "Aesthete, y'know. Wore sandals." I have the feeling that if the new young writers of England heard this judgment now, they would look up from their copies of *Jeeves* and nod their heads in agreement.

I have returned to a literary England where it is sophisticated to show moral disapproval of *Lolita,* and where C. P. Snow's novels are more consistently praised than Lawrence Durrell's or William Golding's, on the grounds that they are "mature" and "responsible." Where one used to condemn a poem by calling it dull, now one simply says that one can't understand it. London is full of bright young men who happily proclaim their incomprehensions.

One *means*, of course, that these poems are deliberately obscure. And one has assumed that they are obscure in order to seem profound, or *avantgarde*, or superior — for modernist art has become associated with social climbing. Although foxhunting country cousins have continued to deride modern art, like their grandfathers who snickered at Sickert, the industrial *nouveaux riches* have acquired imitation cubist masters to go with imitation upper-class accents. By 1950, numerous inhabitants of London and Manchester admired any painter if he was formless enough, any musician if he was noisy enough, and any writer if he was sufficiently confused. One or two publicized poets owe their reputations to this vogue.

The new philistinism — of the intelligent young — starts from the attempt to dissociate English literature from the English class system; the two have been intimately associated for two hundred and fifty years. The newest generation of English writers — in theater, in poetry, in fiction — is nearly unified in repudiating the social accessories of the art. These writers are vigilant in their search for social pretense in writing and in other behavior. They are more honest and self-critical, as a group, than their elders. But the price that they pay is enormous; it is necessary that they resemble their enemy in one important particular: like the lady in my village, they must judge every work of art as a piece of social conduct.

The result can make for ludicrous judgments, especially when the writers concerned are not English. Scots who write in Lallans are treated to vituperation, and their language ignorantly dismissed as affectation. I have heard Samuel Beckett described as if he were trying to be elected to a club. G. S. Fraser, who is certainly one of the better critics in England, called Wallace Stevens a "cultural show-off." Now I doubt very much that by his foreign phrases, obscure terminology, and metaphysical preoccupations, Wallace Stevens was trying to boast that he was more cultured, educated or upperclass than anyone else. Possibly if he had been an insurance executive in England, his literary habits might have had this social meaning. But in Hartford, it didn't apply. A correspondent of the *New Statesman*, writing from New York of the enormous prosperity of abstract expressionist painters, said, "They haven't used it to try and gain a certain social position. One can't imagine them hankering after invitations to smart parties." To an American, even the suggestion is absurd, and it illustrates the social burden the English artist carries.

Any change in critical attitudes necessitates a revision of literary history. Critics have had to invent an "English tradition" which can glide from Hardy through Lawrence and Graves to Philip Larkin without bumping over the mountains of Pound and Eliot. To me, this revision of history is a descent to Little Englandism. It promotes a poetry of daily life — domestic, intimate and minor. R. S. Thomas, a Welsh clergyman, is one of the most celebrated of the recently published poets; he is a small, skillful writer who owes his preeminence to the fashion for the regional and the limited.* Even the "Georgian poets" have come in for reassessment and qualified praise. When I was at Oxford, the epithet implied triviality, incompetence, and sentimentality; it implied everything bad which had been overthrown by the modernist movement.

Of course when good poems are recovered, we can only be grateful. If Edward Thomas was obscured by the

---

*1980: I was wrong to disparage R.S. Thomas.

brilliance of Dylan, we can applaud a restoration of taste that appreciates the older poet. But to discard James Joyce in the process of rediscovering Ralph Hodgson is a stupid waste; and Pound is another author who is largely denounced and unread in England. But mere dismissal is not the only way to invalidate an author as an influence. The prestige of T. S. Eliot is so great that his poetry receives at least lip-service, but when modernist poetry like Eliot's *is* praised, it is usually qualified as not English. Modernism is called a Franco-American movement, and so Eliot or Stevens can be admired by a critic who is unwilling to apply their standards to new English writing. Theorists of the new poetry spend all their time settling its limits, and its limits preclude a major achievement.

If only regional poetry can be written now — or only poetry which comes exclusively from daily situations and emotions — very little good poetry will be written at all, and nothing will be written which we call great. The region as it exists in the work of R. S. Thomas is nearly as dead in England as it is in America. The twentieth century has destroyed true regions, and self-conscious attempts at regionalism are one of the least attractive ways of faking poetry. Alternatively, there is the poetry of semi-detached houses, in which the region devolves to a walled garden and a playpen. Within limits like these, Philip Larkin has made good poems out of Whitsun weddings, photograph albums, and churches visited on bicycles. But he is not good *because* of the limitations of his subject matter; and his limitations will prevent him from achieving the greatness of a poet like T. S. Eliot.

The best poetry of the modern world (in England, Ireland, the United States, South America, Spain, Greece, France, Italy, Germany, and Russia at least) has involved sophistication, cosmopolitanism, and ambition. Sometimes this ambition has included learning, at other times spiritual experimentation, at other times sheer brilliance of thought. Always it has required technical mastery and devotion to art. The disappearance of the local has made the cosmopolitan necessary, and the poet has become the universal artificer. The best young writers of England have resigned from this modern world.

Yet true modernist poetry exists in England, unappreciated because it violates the new provincial conventions. Recently Donald Davie adapted a book-length poem, *The Forests of Lithuania*, from Mickiewicz's *Pan Tadeusz*. The style is intricate and the ambition is European. The best first book in many years is Geoffrey Hill's *For the Unfallen*, but these poems are often difficult because they are intensely concentrated. They sin against the commandments which say that poems must be conversational and modest. Only A. Alvarez of the leading critics has seen Hill's importance, and other reviewers have taken pains to call him "pretentious." The most reviled of better English poets is Charles Tomlinson, who is admired in America where *Seeing is Believing* appeared two years ago; it is just being printed in England this summer. Tomlinson's fault is his modernism, which involves a concern with art that ignores all domestic and intimate subject matters. When Kingsley Amis asked that there be "no more poems about foreign cities," he was indicating the social interpretation by which Tomlinson's aesthetic cosmopolitanism is condemned.

England's literary climate makes it unhealthy for the sort of poetic ambition which we have become used to in the last fifty years. Yet when I compare England to America, there are compensations even in this limitation.

As an Irishman said when he looked out his window at the 27th consecutive day of rain, "I suppose it's better than no climate at all." Where America's intellectual life is diffuse, a matter of Auden's "ironic points of light" if anything at all, England's is centered in London and a few magazines. You can walk easily from the B.B.C. down Regent Street to *Encounter*, across to Charing Cross Road and *The London Magazine*, and up toward Holborn to the *Spectator* and the *New Statesman*. In a pub centrally located among these magazines — and among all the book publishers as well — a group of writers meets every Wednesday at lunch for argument and pints of bitter. It was originally John Wain's day (the Wain's-day lunch) for coming in from Reading, but now that Wain and his bride are trying to gather royalties in Russia, the Wednesdays go on without him. What typifies the writers who gather there (and they do not all subscribe to the heresies I have attributed as a generalization) is their attitude toward the English class system.

Many of them, I feel, do not distinguish between legitimate modernism, and modernism assumed for the sake of social modernism, and modernism assumed for the sake of social climbing. All year long I have been arguing at these Wednesday lunches. England is a country of literary dialogue. When you see an article you disagree with, you can write your letter and start a public fight. Or if you wish, you can go to the pub where the writer hangs out, and make it personal. Controversy seems natural, and people are really writing to other people. In America I have felt that, if I was lucky, I might be writing opinions to be filed in a library for the benefit of researchers. England makes one feel a part of something current. When I wrote an intemperate attack on English provincialism in the *New Statesman*, I was fought over, four days later, at a literary party where half the people who write in England were drinking warm Scotch. It makes you feel that you exist, and that something you have said is worth getting angry about.

The Uses Of Free Verse (1961)

THERE is a rhyme which ends, as I remember it, with a reference to the little magazines "That died to make verse free." The militant controversy over free verse, which raged in literary journals forty years ago, looks quaint from this distance. The manifesto of an Amy Lowell is touching and absurd, because we all include free verse in our private anthologies, and because the best new American poets since 1925 — Ransom, Crane, Tate, Winters, Roethke, Lowell, Wilbur — are practitioners of rhyme and meter.

A few good poets, working from the example of William Carlos Williams, have perfected their individual cadences against the iambic stream; Robert Creeley, Denise Levertov, and Gilbert Sorrentino handle the movement of free verse with consistent brilliance. But there are signs that free verse is reviving in more than a few isolated poets. Recently several young Americans, who used to write metered and rhymed stanzas, have turned to free verse. James Wright and Robert Bly have been writing short, modernist poems on Spanish models. And Robert

Lowell, in *Life Studies*, converted his intense ten-syllable iambics into a free verse that was colloquial and easy.

It's hard to define free verse except by saying what it's free of. Yvor Winters has scanned the accents of free verse, and T. S. Eliot has talked about its structure in terms of its origins. "The ghost of some simple meter," Eliot says, "should lurk behind the arras in even the 'freest' verse."

The form needs to be written in a house haunted by the ghosts of more conventional forms. Or to put it another way, free verse lives on interest from the capital of tradition. But it is not just a parasite, or there would be no reason to write it. There are excellent reasons why poets attempt free verse right now. The necessity which evaporated in 1925 seems to have returned.

Casual readers probably regard free verse as a liberation from restrictive rules, but I think that for many poets free verse is attractive because of its difficulty. It is a liberation from the protective cover of conventional form, a cover which in its easy grace can serve to disguise true feeling. American poets of the last decades made themselves technically enormously proficient. No generation of poets in America has ever been so competent. But competence is a dangerous achievement, and complacency lives next door. Pride of the intellect diminishes into vanity of the craft. Robert Frost has compared making poems to the occupational therapy which helps the insane; you make shapes against chaos. Traditional form — iambic pentameters, ABAB quatrains, metaphors like performing dogs — is a set of techniques for making shapes. If you have practiced with your toolbox you can make shapes out of any material, but the shape of the object may have no useful relation to the material — bracelets out of pigskin, wallets out of silver. Too many poems of the Fifties were merely the application of competent techniques on sugar and water. The results will endure as long as cotton candy.

I don't believe, as Robert Bly does, that history has invalidated the iamb and the rhyme. Nor do I agree with William Carlos Williams that the American language demands a new meter, toward which free verse is reaching. I do believe that for many poets now the devices of traditional form are fatally associated with trivial exercises of craftsmanship. These poets started by struggling with regular forms, but they won the battle and therefore lost the war. By mastering their craft they wore it out. Free verse is always written when the associations of traditional form impede the practice of the art.

Now it is paradoxical to hold that the adoption of a new technique will absolve the poet of his reliance on technique, but the point is that free verse is not *a* technique. Free verse requires a symmetry which is integral, because it allows no symmetry which is merely applicable. Competent conventional form knows how to mimic the shape of feeling, even though the poet tries to impose control by *his* feeling: a rhyme which is witty substitutes by its formal gesture for an exact name; an inversion of the order of stress imitates the precision of true feeling.

Free verse is useful to the poet because it is so difficult. It forces him back on his ear and his imagination. It requires him to return to the primary mystery of making. It obliges him to make a shape which is whole, in which the outer is only the extension of the inner. If he creates a shape against chaos, he knows it is not a skill but an invention. He finds it more difficult to write because he cannot acquire skills, but he finds that by lacking skills he is more able to tell the truth. He had to die before he could be born again.

American Poetry Now (1961)*

F OR thirty years an orthodoxy ruled American poetry. It derived from the authority of T. S. Eliot and the new critics; it exerted itself through the literary quarterlies and the universities. It asked for a poetry of symmetry, intellect, irony, and wit. The last few years have broken the control of this orthodoxy. The change has come slowly and not as a rebellion of young turks against old tories. For one thing, the orthodoxy produced many good poems and some of its members are still producing them. For another, much of the attack on it came from sources — like *Time* and the publicists of the Beat Generation — which could not supply literary alternatives to the orthodoxy.

Yet we must not regret the dissolution of the old government. In modern art anarchy has proved preferable to the restrictions of a benevolent tyranny. It is preferable as a permanent condition. We do not want merely to substitute one orthodoxy for another — Down with

*An introduction to the Penguin *Contemporary American Poetry*.

Understanding Poetry! Long Live *Projective Verse!* — but we want all possibilities, even contradictory ones, to exist together. The trouble with orthodoxy is that it prescribes the thinkable limits of variation; among young poets of the forties and fifties, almost without exception, surrealism was quite literally beyond consideration. The orthodoxy which prevailed in every literary context had decided, while the poet was still in short pants, that "surrealism had failed." And that was the end of that. Yet typically the modern artist has allowed nothing to be beyond his consideration. He has acted as if restlessness were a conviction and has destroyed his own past in order to create a future. He has said to himself, like the policeman to the vagrant, "Keep moving."

Modern American poetry began in London shortly after the death of Queen Victoria. Ezra Pound recalls that Conrad Aiken told him that there was "a guy at Harvard doing funny stuff. Mr. Eliot turned up a year or so later." Harriet Monroe founded *Poetry* in 1912, and discovered Mr. Pound on her neck encouraging her to print Eliot, Frost, and Yeats. But soon after the first successes of modernist poetry in America, when Amy Lowell was flying the flag of revolution, the modernists split into opposing camps. One side of this split became the orthodoxy that prevailed from, say, 1925 to 1955.

In the first decades of this century there were the expatriates and there were the poets who remained in the United States. Pound, Aiken, and Eliot congregated in London, but things were also going on in New York. Poets and editors like Alfred Kreymbourg, Mina Loy, William Carlos Williams, Marianne Moore, Wallace Stevens, E.E. Cummings, and Hart Crane mingled and established a domestic literary milieu. They shared little but liveliness and talent, but most of them also experimented with the use of common American speech, an indigenous language increasingly distinguishable from English. Even the frenchified Wallace Stevens and the rhetorical Hart Crane participated in this endeavor. And none of these New York poets shared the concern with history which occupied Eliot and Pound, or the erudition which this concern imposed.

Pound was the link between London and Greenwich Village, as editor and publicist and even as poet. But he was unable to reconcile the slangy Williams and the polyglot Eliot. And it was the ideas of Eliot which proved attractive to the young men who took power. According to William Carlos Williams in his *Autobiography*, "The *Waste Land* wiped out our world... Eliot returned us to the classroom." Eliot was never further from a colloquial language than at the end of the most famous poem of our modern literature:

> *London bridge is falling down falling down falling down*
> Poi s'ascose nel foco che gli affina
> Quando fiam uti chelidon — *O swallow swallow*
> Le Prince d'Aquitaine à la tour abolie
> *These fragments I have shored against my ruins*
> *Why then Ile fit you. Hieronymo's mad againe.*
> *Datta. Dayadhvam. Damyata.*
> **Shantih shantih shantih**

It was not only a matter of language, however; and in some of his poems Eliot certainly used a vocabulary and a rhythm which were close to common American speech. Eliot's attitudes towards history and tradition were more deeply relevant, as well as his sense of the continuity of American and English poetry. Probably his influence was largely accomplished through his criticism. From the mid-twenties until very recently, American poetry has functioned as a part of the English tradition. The colloquial side of American literature — the side which valued "experience" more than "civilization" — was neglected by the younger poets. Melville said that the whaleboats of the Pacific had been his Harvard and his Yale College; Henry James crossed the Atlantic from Harvard to Lamb House. The directions are as contrary as East and West.

The new poets admired the forms of the sixteenth and seventeenth centuries, and themselves attempted to write a symmetrical and intellectual poetry which resembled Ralegh or Dryden more than "Gerontion" or the *Cantos*. One can divide the chief poets of this time into those who admired the tough density of Donne, and those who preferred the wit of Marvell or the delicacy of Herrick. There were Allen Tate and Yvor Winters on the one hand, and there was John Crowe Ransom on the other. Late in the thirties another group of poets took their departure most obviously from Auden — Karl Shapiro and John Frederick Nims were the best, I think — but because their poems were witty and formal they did not depart from the general area of the orthodoxy.

Immediately after the war, two books were published which were culminations of the twin strains of density and delicacy. Robert Lowell's *Lord Weary's Castle* is a monument of the line of tough rhetoricians; beyond this it was impossible to go. (The failure of John Berryman's *Homage to Mistress Bradstreet*, as I see it, only proves my point.) The effect of tremendous power under tremendous pressure was a result of a constricted subject matter and a

tense line, in which the strict decasyllable was counter-
balanced by eccentric caesura and violent enjambement.
In contrast was Richard Wilbur's *The Beautiful Changes*,
which was the peak of skillful elegance. Here was the
ability to shape an analogy, to perceive and develop comparisons, to display etymological wit, and to pun six ways
at once. It appealed to the mind because it was intelligent,
and to the sense of form because it was intricate and
shapely. It did not appeal to the passions and it did not
pretend to. These two poets, though they are not the
oldest here, form the real beginning of post-war American
poetry because they are the culmination of past poetries.

Lowell had his imitators, but they were not very
successful because Lowell's style was idiosyncratic. Many
poets after Wilbur resembled him, and some of them were
good at it, but the typical *ghastly* poem of the fifties was a
Wilbur poem not written by Wilbur, a poem with tired wit
and obvious comparisons and nothing to keep the mind or
the ear occupied. (It wasn't Wilbur's fault, though I expect he will be asked to suffer for it.) The *poème bien fait*,
which filled the quarterlies of the fifties, was usually not
that damned *bien fait*. Too often it sounded like:

Also the wind assumed the careful day
And down the avenues of hollow light
The sons of Jupiter to their dismay
Perceived the ritual desuetude of night.

The real subject of these poems was the faint music of
their diction. They were decadent products of the old
move toward irony, wit, and control. The experiments of
1927 became the cliches of 1952. American poetry, which
has always been outrageous — compare Whitman and

Dickinson to Browning and Tennyson — dwindled into long poems in iambics called "Harakles: A double Sestina." Myth, myth, myth. Jung was perhaps influential, but what distinguished these poems from the fables of Edwin Muir was that they existed in order to *prevent* meaning. Nobody could pin them down. Sometimes it seemed that the influence of Senator McCarthy was stronger than that of Jung.

Meanwhile a series of contrary directions in poetry had existed in semi-obscurity. The vanguard *New Directions* annuals printed some of them, and others survived in little mimeographed magazines and home-made pamphlets. Most of these underground poems were bad, like most poems anywhere, but they were bad in ways differing from the prevailing badness. In the thirties there was a brief upsurge of surrealism, which produced nothing. There was also a certain amount of Marxist poetry, some of it publicized, but except for the sarcasms of Kenneth Fearing little of it was readable.

The only contrary direction which endured throughout the orthodoxy was the direction I will inadequately call the colloquial, or the line of William Carlos Williams. Williams himself has been admired by most new American poets, of whatever school, but the poets of the orthodoxy have admired him for his descriptive powers; they learned from him a conscience of the eye rather than a conscience of the ear; for Williams the problem of native speech rhythm was of first importance.

This poetry is no mere restriction of one's vocabulary. It wants to use the language with the intimacy acquired in unrehearsed unliterary speech. But it has no other characteristics which are not linguistic. It is a poetry of experiences more than of ideas. The experience is presented often without comment, and the words of the description must supply the emotion which the experience generates, without generalization or summary. Often too this poetry finds great pleasure in the world outside. It is the poetry of a man in the world, responding to what he sees: with disgust, with pleasure, in rant and in meditation. Naturally, this colloquial direction makes much of accuracy, of honest speech. "Getting the tone right" is the poet's endeavor, not "turning that metaphor neatly" or "inventing a new stanza." Conversely, when it fails most commonly it fails because the emotion does not sound true.

People who had learned from Williams, and from Pound's structure and metric, had a hard time of it until the fifties. Then some good editors began to print the best of them, and the movement which had lapsed in the twenties came alive again. Cid Corman started *Origin* in 1951, and printed many of the best poems written in this tradition. Jonathan Williams started the Jargon Press in North Carolina, and printed good poets who were later picked up by New York publishers. I will not try to discriminate among the various poets who belong, some quite loosely, to this strain of American literature. Denise Levertov is from England, Robert Creeley from Massachusetts, and Robert Duncan from California; the sources of their poetry are probably as varied as their geographical origins. All of these poets and many more pay tribute to an older poet named Charles Olson, who in his letters and articles and poems (though he did not begin publishing until the fifties) erected a critical standard for them. But one thing unites them all: an alternative to the traditional poetry of the last decades was necessary, and was implicit in the nature of America; a Henry James demands a Herman Melville, and English influence begets a French antagonist.

When he wrote *Life Studies*, Robert Lowell sent his muse to the *atelier* of William Carlos Williams. Many of the poets of the orthodoxy have felt the need to move on, to change. Earlier than Lowell, Richard Eberhart and Theodore Roethke moved from their original old models to new unorthodoxies. (Others, like Richard Wilbur, are staying put, and there is no reason why a man should change if he doesn't feel like changing. There is Ezra Pound but there is also Robert Frost.) I suggested that *Lord Weary's Castle* was the culmination of one movement. *Life Studies* looks like an attempt at synthesis. If the poet of rhetorical stanzas can come closer to common speech, he may avoid the mere fabrication of mandalas into available shapes. The challenge of free verse is to make shapes which derive their identity by improvisation, without reference to past poems. And also, a new form can uncover or make possible a new subject matter. Synthesis of the literary and the colloquial occurs, surely, in some of the poets of the vanguard already. An approach of the two contraries may guard against the perversions of each.

I have not mentioned another group of poets who are sufficiently separate. (I have not mentioned the Beat Generation, incidentally, because it is an invention of weekly news magazines. Insofar as it has made several good lines of poetry, it has belonged to the colloquial tradition.) These are a group of New Yorkers who have been associated with Action Painting — some have worked for *Art News*, or the Museum of Modern Art — and whose poetry attempts a similar vitality. Their closeness to modern French poetry seems obvious. Frank O'Hara, with his *Second Avenue*, comes closest to Action Writing. But the best of these poets, it seems to me, is John Ashbery, whom I print here.

Most of my comments have limited themselves to the terms of technique, like vocabulary and symmetrical form. One needs to wear certain spectacles, if one is to see everything at once. But you will notice that I repeat the eternal American tic of thinking about art in terms of its techniques. (This tic is shared by left wing and right wing and middle.) We talk about syllabics or sestinas or a colloquial vocabulary or old spelling as if they made up a Little Marvel Poetry Kit, Free 10-day offer, One to a Customer, No Home Without It. The danger is that we may take technical variations more seriously than they warrant. We could argue that the movement which Robert Lowell typifies, from *Lord Weary's Castle* to *Life Studies*, is only a movement from one style of the twenties to another, from Allen Tate to William Carlos Williams, and that it is retrospective. If it makes it new, it makes it new within Lowell only.

One thing is happening in American poetry, as I see it, which is genuinely new, and so new that I lack words for it. In lines like Robert Bly's:

In small towns the houses are built right on the ground;
The lamplight falls on all fours in the grass.

or Louis Simpson's:

These houses built of wood sustain
Colossal snows,
And the light above the street is sick to death.

a new kind of imagination seems to be working. The vocabulary is mostly colloquial but the special quality of the lines has nothing to do with an area of diction; it is quality learned neither from T. S. Eliot nor William Carlos Williams. This imagination is irrational yet the poem is usually quiet and the language simple; there is no straining for apocalypse and no conscious pursuit of the unconscious. There is an inwardness to these images, a profound subjectivity. Yet they are not subjective in the autobiographical manner of *Life Studies* or *Heart's Needle*, which are confessional and particular. This new imagination reveals through images a subjective life which is *general*, and which corresponds to an old objective life of shared experience and knowledge.

The later poems of James Wright provide more examples of this new imagination. Among other poets in this volume, whose verse forms associate them with one or another poetical faction, I find the same quality scattered — an unacknowledged content. What I am trying to describe is not a school or a clique but a way of seeing and a way of feeling, and I believe they have grown by themselves from the complex earth of American writing and American experience.

* * * * * * * *

1980: My original introduction to the Penguin *Contemporary American Poets* ended as above. Two years after the first publication of the anthology, when Penguin was about to reprint it, the editor asked me if I had any changes to make. In the meantime, I had found some new "words for it," and I took advantage of Penguin's offer:

One thing is happening in American poetry, as I see it, which is genuinely new, and so new that I lack words for it. In lines like Robert Bly's:

In small towns the houses are built right on the ground;
The lamplight falls on all fours in the grass.

or Louis Simpson's:

The clouds are lifting from the high Sierras,
The Bay mists clearing;
And the angel in the gate, the flowering plum,
Dances like Italy, imagining red.

there is a kind of imagination new to American poetry. The vocabulary is mostly colloquial, but the special quality of the lines has nothing to do with an area of diction; it is a quality learned neither from T. S. Eliot nor William Carlos Williams. It is a quality closer to the spirit of Georg Trakl or Pablo Neruda, but it is not to be pigeon-holed according to any sources. This imagination is irrational, yet the poem is usually quiet and the language simple; there is no straining after apocalypse. There is an inwardness to these images, a profound subjectivity. Yet they are not subjective in the autobiographical manner of *Life Studies* or *Heart's Needle*, which are confessional and particular. Confessional poetry is certainly a widespread manner now in the United States. Snodgrass and Lowell were followed by Anne Sexton, and most effectively by Sylvia Plath in the remarkable poems she wrote before her death in 1963. Like any movement, confessional poetry has bred imitators swarming among the magazines. What began as a series of excruciating self-discoveries — often

professionally aided by therapist or analyst — dissipates in
an orgy of exhibitionism.

The movement which seems to me *new* is subjective but
not autobiographical. It reveals through images not particular pain, but general subjective life. This universal
subjective corresponds to the old objective life of shared
experience and knowledge. People can talk to each other
most deeply in images. To read a poem of this sort, you
must not try to translate the images into abstractions.
They won't go. You must try to be open to them, to let
them take you over and speak in their own language of
feeling. It is the intricate darkness of feeling and instinct
which these poems mostly communicate. The poems are
best described as expressionist: like the painter, the poet
uses fantasy and distortion to express feeling. The poet
may hesitate, when he is looking for a word, between opposites; would "tiny" or "huge" be better here?, "mountain" or "valley"? Such hesitation shows the irrationality
and the arbitrariness of this method, but it does not imply
that one of the alternatives is not enormously more appropriate than the other — only that neither is literal. The
reader or the poet cannot go to the outside world and
check — Ah, yes, the Empire State Building is "huge," not
"tiny" — but we are not concerned with accuracy to exter-
nals; he can only make a subjective check with his inward
world. When the painter hesitates between blue and green
for the lady's face, he is at least certain that he will not
paint it flesh-color.

Poems Without Legs (1963)*

C OLIN FALK was talking the other day about "poems
without legs." I think this describes exactly what I
want in poetry now, and what Robert Bly and James
Wright, for instance, are doing.

*The best of these poems do have legs which one can
define as dramatic legs: they concern themselves with an
area of activity which is generally shared and generally
agreed upon...*

Maybe I should say "poems without crutches" because
they will not all necessarily lack some thread of narrative
or conventional discourse, but they won't depend on it;

---

*1980: This interview took place at Oxford in 1963, and
makes reference to the introduction to the Penguin anthology.
In italics there are questions and remarks by J.R.S. Davies, Bill
Byrom, and Ian Hamilton. I began by quoting Colin Falck, an
English poet and critic, who was quoting William Empson, who
was *not* praising poems as double amputees.

71

their real energy will come not from the conventional structure of the poem, but from the images themselves as they are juxtaposed. A "poem without legs" does not rely on these old methods of construction which have come to turn the poem into, for the most part, a kind of "argument" poem.

Yes, but at the same time in their theory they do talk about irrational poetry springing from a rational source . . . It seems to me in some ways that what they are saying is related to a total attitude to the world — it's impossible to say things about the world, it's impossible even to use ordinary descriptions because these descriptions might not be true . . .

At the beginning of Bly's book of poems* that came out in America last year, there is a quotation from Jacob Boehme: "We are all asleep in the outward man." The only "real" world is the world that we all share unconsciously, inwardly. This is the world to which poetry really must make reference. Of course, this is a startling thing in the context of English and American poetry in the last thirty years. American poetry has been so concerned with *things:* English poetry has concerned itself with replacing the informal essay — writing occasional poems, poems that are bits and pieces of the objective world. These poems have nothing to do with Imagism or Objectivism, technically, but spiritually they are identical. If you look back at what T. E. Hulme says at the start of the modern movement, it is all an attempt to move poetry out-

---

Silence in the Snowy Fields, Wesleyan University Press, 1962.

side, towards getting in facts, opinions and generalizations. Poetry is becoming impoverished by facts. The poetry we're talking about now concerns itself with fantasy, with imagination. . . I think Bly is a revolutionary, but the revolution that he wants is an inward one, not an exterior one. When that revolution takes place then we shall see the Shell-stations in a new light, as in his poem "The Possibility of New Poetry." When that revolution comes there is social change because he believes that the inward world contains a way of feeling which changes our exterior actions. In Bly's poems, the recognition of this interior world and the employment of imagination is in itself a criticism of the world of bourgeois capitalists. It happens when you allow the imagination to work so that you have metamorphoses and strange connections. For instance, another poem of Bly's, "After the Industrial Revolution, All Things Happen at Once" — all these things are bits of the exterior world, yes, but putting them together is an act of the imagination. Putting them together without conjunctions, without any legs.

But he's not just putting them together, he's putting them one after another: surely that implies a time sequence?

I don't think so. In literature we are always cursed with the necessity to put one thing after another, but increasingly modern writers have wanted to cancel out time and work for simultaneity. By omitting conjunctions, anything that makes things go together — this would include the order of logic — by omitting these things, one gets a sense of duplication and therefore simultaneity.

One moves toward simultaneity even though the art of literature is necessarily a time art, an art of sequence.

I was interested in something someone said when I spoke to the Poetry Society here — "You want, then a poetry without conjunction?" I agreed that conjunctions would not be part of my poetry because I wanted the sense of simultaneity, the kind of effect you get from juxtaposing things without leading the reader to a particular kind of intellectual relationship among them. But later I realized perhaps I would like the kind of conjunctions that don't make any sense by acting to deny the sense of conjunction. I mean, you say that the grass is green because — there was a fire yesterday in Timbuctoo. That ridicules conjunctionism. In the same way narrative "legs" can be used to make a nonsensical narrative which itself can be a narrative of imagination.

This new poetry will open the floodgates to a lot of crap, surely?

Definitely! Any new poetry will — even Wordsworth opened the floodgates to a lot of crap. . . .

Yes, but it's very difficult to work out ways in which you begin to discriminate between kinds of nonsense. . . Since we are talking in theoretical terms, I find what I'm troubled by is the permissive element in this theory.

It is a danger, and a danger that I am perfectly happy to undertake for the sake of the possible gains. I think you are right in implying that there are probably more possible ways to fail here — because the judgment that one can give to this kind of poem is not really analytical. No, this kind of poem takes assent or dissent. You either say yes to it or you say — crap.

But it seems to me the more you particularize in your dream world the more eccentric it's going to seem. The more you allow it to turn on grand absolutes of light and dark the more you keep to this very general sort of abstract center. But the more you give it some kind of individual particularity, the more it's likely to be written in a sort of egocentric eccentric dream world.

Are you saying that you approve of a more general kind. . .?

But, I mean, if it has to turn on abstracts, it also turns on clichés. . . .

I suspect that what you say is really false and that there are more sets of symbols and interior references with a generalizable meaning available to poets if they dig deeply enough. One need not go to the eccentric, to the merely individual, to find them. I think that the difficulty with this kind of poetry for most people is that they apply a kind of reading inappropriate to the poem. You must lay yourself open to the poem and not translate as you go along. You must try to accept the images into yourself and let them happen. You must try not to resist eccentricity, but find in yourself a response to the images.

Are these poems constructed like any other English or American poems that you can think of?

Take a little poem by James Wright — "Lying In a Hammock. . ." — which starts out with the poet lying in a hammock seeing certain things — turds, horses' droppings, "blaze into golden stones." Now that has absolutely nothing to do with the kind of discourse that people like Philip Larkin wish to enter into — it has no apparent relationship to the last line, "I have wasted my life." Finally one can go back and see that everything is changing in the poem and that everything he's looking at is somehow getting better — even turds are blazing into golden stones — except him. The distance between the droppings of horses and a man lying in a hammock is so extraordinary a distance — compared with, for instance, in Larkin's "The Whitsun Weddings," the poet alone and all the other chaps married. The huge imaginative leap from the one thing to another is close enough to having no legs. . . .

Images are the units of speech from one unconscious mind to another. With an objective image one feels visual (or aural, or whatever) recognition: yes, that's the way it looks. With the "interior" image, the subject is not anything in the exterior world; the subject is a feeling — something as general as that — a feeling, a sense. A poem can be united by the title "Miners," it can be united by a subject which is implicit without the title. Obviously, it must have some form, some sort of unity — it must provide a sense of *completion*. It has to be improvised out of images towards a sense of completion without depending, primarily, at any rate, upon the legs of logical discourse or narrative.

Wouldn't you say that, for instance, Wright's poem on

Eisenhower's visit to Franco was using a traditional ironic structure?

I wouldn't describe the poem that way at all. It seems to work on contrast, yes. Now Cleanth Brooks generalizes irony so much that practially anything that contrasts is irony. I mean, if you mention light, then dark, ah, that's ironic. But I don't think that's a very useful idea of irony.

But if you contrast politicians like Franco with the sort of poor people....

That's not irony, is it?

Well, here light applies to all the glittering that's going on in Madrid with the planes arriving: the dark is in respect of the poor people and yet Franco is promising that all dark things will be hunted down. By which he means something quite different from what the poem implies by dark.

I don't think he does. I think the poet regards him as being the enemy of all those things that he calls dark. Franco is the enemy of "the mouths of old men," the enemy of wine and so on. If you think that that's ironic language because light is usually assumed to be good and dark bad, well, then we have to throw out a lot of Blake and a lot of Lawrence — no, not throw them out, but consider that they were being ironical! I think Wright is taking light quite clearly. The metallic kind of light and glitter that he's talking about is a bad thing.

It's been perverted, surely?

77

It's a bad thing, while everything about the dark is good. I don't see any irony. Irony seems to me to happen when you use light honorifically and then let it sneak in finally that light is not all that seems, that light has its dark side.

I mean, I thought he was playing on the traditional properties of light etcetera associated with virtue and showing that in this case. . .

He's not doing it here because there is a huge modern tradition to establish the goodness of dark things. And this comes immediately to mind when one sees how he's doing it. One doesn't have any sense, "Oh, he means light to be dark this time, how clever of him." The way I see the poem, it works on a series of *expressive* images in contrast. There is no double-take of any kind. Irony always seems to me to employ a double-take and a moment of uncertainty before one sees where the real force lies. The beauty of these images seems to me that they are absolutely clear in their effect from the moment they are uttered. And their effect is the whole point of them; they're expressionist images. We have simple sets of contrasts, delicately worked out, and the result is a marvelous impeachment, a real political statement in which, the world of the imagination — is a judgment upon the world of metallic light. We have had so many *terrible* anti-fascist poems, for God's sake, and the reason most of them are terrible is that the opposition, the thing that we have to be anti-fascist *from*, is something as weak as doing good or being nice to people. The usual liberalism. In this poem we don't have that: we have the other side of it — the darkness, the wine in the mouths of old men — contained in images. . . .

Writers In The Universities (1965)*

FOR A century or two, poets made their living as vicars
or citizens of Grub Street. In England at the moment
many poets work for advertising agencies — the newest
Grub Street — which display volumes of staff-written
verse in their foyers for prestige. But in America, writers
inhabit the vicarages of university English departments.

Despite the examples of Longfellow and Robert Frost,
universities did not generally accord writers respectability
until after World War II. (Pioneers in the thirties, like Yvor
Winters and Allen Tate, ran into resistance from old-line
professors of English.) Now fashion has changed; any
serious writer — serious does not mean good — who
publishes regularly can make his living from colleges or
universities. Departments of English have come to expect
a writer on the staff just as they expect Blue Cross and
cocktail parties. Recently, the poet-teachers at two
middle-sized Eastern universities died at about the same

---

*1980: This essay was written for an *Atlantic Monthly* symposium on the American university.

time. The Poet was dead; long live the Poet. Both universities competed for the services of a young replacement who had just won a prize for his first book.

Writer-teachers generally teach an ordinary academic schedule. I get irritated when people introduce me as the poet in residence of the University of Michigan. I'm not. A poet in residence doesn't teach any courses. He is a poet who is in residence on campus, and if he is generous, he talks to undergraduates from time to time. But *who* is he? I don't know of any permanent poet in residence at the present time. Some colleges call their English department poet by this phrase, perhaps to avoid the embarrassment of giving an academic title to someone without a Ph.D., but they work him as a professor. One man I know was granted rank equivalent to associate professor but the title of associate in poetry. (I love prepositions like that "in.") Other writers do have Ph.D.'s, and some have even become chairmen of their departments: William Stafford at Lewis and Clark and J. V. Cunningham at Brandeis.

A good many producing writers, on the other hand, are granted some relief from extra chores, and special scheduling of their classes, in order to give them more time to write. Though they are not merely "in residence," they are more fortunate than other teachers. Like experimental physicists and rare scholars, they are allowed privileges denied the less productive.

Of course the vogue for writer-teachers leads to silliness. Most English professors, like most publishers and book reviewers, can't tell a good new writer from a bad new writer at a distance of five years. Recently, a really bad poet — I'm not being catty about a rival; I mean someone truly incompetent, like a center fielder who hits .124 in class D baseball (but an artist can never be *sure,* and can always find someone like his mother to praise him and something like the *New York Times* editorial page that will publish him) — decided to look for a teaching job. He mimeographed a list of the newspapers in which he had published and the titles of the books had had printed for himself, and sent it to all the colleges in the almanac. He is now an associate professor of English at a bad college in New England, where his ability goes un-questioned as his poems go unread.

I have been talking about the writer as a fixed part of the university, the writer with a regular job; I will refer to him as the Fixed Writer, with only the slightest suggestion that he may be fixed like a dog or a cat. There is also the Rotating Writer, who visits a variety of campuses for varying lengths of time. (Many Fixed Writers rotate on their days off, and resemble their colleagues in physics and business administration who supplement their salaries with consultation fees from industry.) The most common phenomenon is the poetry reading, where the Rotating Poet spends approximately a day on campus, do-ing a reading and often taking a class or two, as well as having lunch with the English department and tea with the English club. Many of these readings are instigated when a department member who is enthusiastic about the work of a poet writes him a letter. Others are organized into the Poetry Circuits, set up by Elizabeth Kray of the Academy of American Poets. Here, anywhere from eight to twenty colleges in a given area form a potential se-quence for a poet, who takes a small fee for each appearance ($100) but makes up for it by volume. The colleges share his expenses and get a poet for the cut-rate price of about $120. There are circuits in North Carolina, Michigan, Ohio, two in New York State, a large one in the central Midwest, one in New England, and others in the process of being born. Professional lecture agencies handle other poets: English ones like Cecil Day Lewis, expensive ones like W. H. Auden, and some who are not so expensive; you can buy a genuine poet for $500. Many colleges small and large have convocations and arts festivals and all manner of occasions for Rotating Writers. Opportunities to rotate are growing, and so are lecture fees. Some universities like to have a writer come to stay for a week or two, reading and talking and being available to students, and pay him accordingly. Writers who perform well on the platform are beginning to discover that they can make as much in six weeks on the road as they can in nine months of teaching.*

When a university hires a Fixed Writer, one of its motives is visibility. Visibility is an academic euphemism for publicity. Competition for grants, for faculty, for graduate students, and even for the best undergraduate students requires that the university appear in the public eye. Budgets of state legislatures provide an obvious annual crisis, but private institutions are just as much concerned: alumni are interested in visibility, too. After a basketball player on the cover of *Sports Illustrated* or a physicist who becomes a Nobel Laureate, a National Book Award novelist comes a decent third. (Academic attention paid to prizes, most of which are rubber medals, is extraordinary; a good poet I know, who was seldom asked to do readings, read at fifty-five universities the year after he won the Pulitzer.) But even when a writer is not a prizewinner, by definition he *publishes.* Some good and dedicated teachers have to struggle, against their in-

---

*1980: These words emerged from boom times.

clinations, to publish in order not to perish academically; the writer as long as he remains a writer is building his bibliography simply by being what he is. The biographical note at the back of the magazine states that Mr. X is a professor at Y University, and the dean of the college smiles. It is possible that the professional writer may benefit his unproductive colleagues by accumulating bibliography in the dean's office, the way Nuns of Perpetual Adoration store up prayers for souls in purgatory.

But the university writer is a teacher too, and as a teacher the university may look for a number of special things from him. In most departments, the writer-teacher has classes in literature as well as in writing.* When he teaches literature, the intelligent writer looks upon it with a more technical eye, as a shape constructed by a series of possible choices, than does the professor of Victorian literature who finds "Dover Beach" (1) a monolith and (2) a document of intellectual history. His approach is more critical and formal, less biographical and historical. Not to argue the value of these biases, the university should find it valuable to represent them all. The writer lends humanity to the study of literature, first by his dynamic attitude toward the art as a piece of making, and second, by his mere presence as a man engaged in the struggle to make art. He helps the undergraduate to think of Shakespeare not as a monument, but as a man who sat with a piece of paper and solved problems.

------

*1980: I am not sure that this was true when I said it. Deplorably, it is untrue now. "Creative Writing" often takes its separate corner, with bad results for writers, students and English Departments.

Then there is "creative writing" — a presumptuous phrase. I am still astonished at the people who, having discovered that one teaches such a course, smirk and ask, "But can you *really* teach people to be poets?" The answer is, "*Of course not*, you bloody fool!"...but you can teach a great deal else in a course in which students try to make poems and stories. Mere talent is common; what is rare is eudurance, the continuing desire to work hard at writing. What is rarest is originality or achievement. Perhaps I have taught two hundred would-be writers at Michigan. I think as many as eighty had talent. At least twenty have printed in *Poetry*, *The Nation*, *The Hudson Review*, *New Statesman*, The *Times Literary Supplement*, the *New Yorker*. There are three who I think will be writers for the rest of their lives. And of them I would be rash to predict anything further.

But I feel no frustration, because I have taught most of these students more, I suspect, than I have taught a random two hundred of my literature students. I have taught them something about understanding literature that they would not have learned otherwise. The practice of writing, provided that you have a minimal ability to put one word after another, is an immeasurable help toward the intimate reading of literature. By accomplishing even wooden versification, one learns to scan; by confronting one's own metaphorical mishmash, one learns to distinguish the metaphorical genius of a master. So the university hires in a writer-teacher a special exponent of the teaching of literature.

But the convention of the writer-teacher is not always so happy for the university as I make it sound. The reason some well-known writers keep moving from place to place is not so much being restless as being arrested. But more

84

commonly, the writer is an egotist who has a loyalty to himself which transcends his loyalty to his students. He will hold back from his students in order to preserve strength for his own endeavors. He will not sacrifice his art for his teaching, and since teaching involves self-sacrifice, he will be incomplete as a teacher. He will also withhold himself from his colleagues, and will refuse to serve (or will serve lazily) on a committee to which he could otherwise contribute.

Of course there are writers who are conscientious teachers. Theodore Roethke seemed to give himself totally to a class and totally to a poem. But many writers cannot split themselves: either they hold back or they find that their own problems and ambitions disappear beneath the problems and ambitions of their students. They cease being writers and become teachers only, which is not why the university hired them. One well-known novelist, author of three novels, the last of them twelve years old, told me that when he was writing he would wake up in the middle of the night thinking about a piece of his novel; when he was teaching he would wake up in the middle of the night solving a student's problem.

But I have been talking only about the Fixed Writer. The Rotating Writer also fulfills a number of functions for the university. The Arts Festival, fatuous with panels during which writers are expected to toss dirty words at each other, sometimes makes an attempt at visibility. But usually the encounter is single and intramural, a university Cultural Event like a traveling soprano.

When the lecturer or campus visitor is well chosen, there can be a real meeting, which can be intense, and valuable though brief. Whether the occasion is an enforced convocation or a small gathering of the literary club, the Rotating Writer if he is clever can encounter the young student directly and present his own poems and ideas about poetry and literature. He can stimulate both students and faculty. In some colleges one gets asked what's happened since Vachel Lindsay; the visiting writer brings news, and to the naive student he brings evidence that poems are written on purpose. A typical question after reading: "You mean you *mean* those hidden meanings?" If the campus is larger and more sophisticated — if, for instance, there is already a writer on the staff — the visiting writer often brings controversy and the excitement of alternatives to the local orthodoxy. The ideal university is rich enough to have staff writer-teachers, visitors who come for a week or two, and others who fly in for a fast day of talk and fly away again.

As the university wants visibility and a presence, the writer wants solvency and time. The economics of poetry is common scandal. Novelists, until they write *Herzog* or *Ship of Fools*, are in the same position. Unless writers choose bohemianism or poverty — which are real alternatives but involve the sacrifice of desires (family, house, food and drink, books) that are real and strong for many writers — they must make their living in some way other than by writing what they like. They can try writing what they *don't* like — a difficult task to accomplish well — or they can take some sort of regular job.

Teaching has become the regular job usually chosen, for good reasons. Many writers find manual labor onerous, business compromising, advertising dishonest, and publishing a frustrating combination of business and art. There is satisfaction in teaching, and there are also practical advantages to the writer in the nature of the job.

The hours of work are relatively adaptable, since so much of it — preparing classes, grading themes — is done on your own schedule. The amount of work is often adjustable, too: one novelist I know teaches just two courses, at two-thirds pay, and finds that the arrangements leaves him the right amount of time. Others are able to teach full-time one term a year and have eight months each year for uninterrupted writing. But most important, teaching is the one profession from which it is possible to take frequent leave and to return without penalty.

But there are disadvantages to teaching. At first you learn by overhearing yourself be brilliant; later, there is the badness of hearing your voice be brilliant the same way the fifteenth time. Of course, this problem is endemic to teaching and not peculiar to writer-teachers, but I think that it is particularly dangerous to them. When conviction is forced, the voice turns false, and his honest voice is a writer's stock-in-trade. And it is not only the repetitions which hurt the voice; deference hurts it, deference from students and even from colleagues. Undergraduates of moderate intelligence are likely to consider you Shakespeare and Tolstoy; you do not necessarily believe them, but you cannot help smiling as you deny the allegation. In general, even intelligent students look upon you as an authority. For that matter, you are, which is why you were hired in the first place, but authority implies definitive statements from platforms. Poetry comes from meditation, from conversation, even from arguments with friends; it does not come from lectures or from consultations.

There is also the problem of getting on with your colleagues. Deference to the face is often a symptom of sneers behind the back. Though English departments must have their poet, they don't have to like him too. The writer finds considerable hostility, though most of it resides just below the surface of politeness. Some of the trouble is mere jealousy. The writer publishes without struggle and gets paid for it. The writer more often spends a Guggenheim year in Europe. The writer saves up his lecture fees in order to take a term off to write. So a colleague gets drunk at a party and tells the writer's wife. "*Gee*, Fred is a *swell guy*, but why does he *sell out?*" A friend of mine who teaches at a large university in the West made his academic name by writing four critical books. Just recently he brought out a collection of poems he had quietly accumulated over the years. It was well reviewed, and suddenly he was a poet rather than a scholar. I met him, and he smiled happily: "They've stopped talking to me in the corridors!"

For these reasons and others, many writers are looking for a way out of teaching, and some of them find it in rotating — making a living on the road. For years popular critics have complained that modern poets lacked an audience. The Rotating Poet *sees* an audience, hears them laugh and clap, or rustle and cough when they are bored. Reading a new poem to an audience is a form of publication; by the very enunciating of it, the poet may see flaws in it. The vogue of poetry readings — given a boost by Dylan Thomas after the war, but surely reaching back in the American consciousness to Emerson and his colleagues who left the pulpit for the road — grants the poet a memorable audience of true faces, maybe five thousand faces a year. It is still the university which supports him, but the Rotating Writer avoids some of the drawbacks of regular teaching. He is also likely, being a writer, to enjoy performing. He is also likely to make the same money as a Fixed Writer in less time and free himself for more writing.

While the most prominent Fixed Writers leave their jobs in order to rotate, the absolute number of openings for Fixed Writers increases with the growth of universities. There are at least two results. Young writers are hired with magazine publication as their credentials in lieu of a Ph.D. who would once have needed either the Ph.D. or a book of poems. Many of them are thus able to avoid the graduate school years which tortured a generation of American writers. But also, the demand for writers exceeds the supply of real ones; increasingly the fourth-rate writer, who probably cannot teach either, is hired on the basis of wretched, minimal publication. These products of creative-writing classes, returned to teach creative writing, may eventually disgrace the whole convention of the writer-teacher and force the writer to look elsewhere than the university for patronage. Perhaps this moment has come to pass.*

---

*1980: Jobs for writers have dried up as poetry readings have dried up. Take from this essay the complacencies of prosperity, and the outline remains valid.

It took me until 1975 to leave the university, and it was not rotating that did it. It was of course a textbook.

An Ethic Of Clarity (1968)*

EZRA POUND, George Orwell, James Thurber, and Ernest Hemingway don't have much in common: a great poet who became a follower of Mussolini, a disillusioned left-wing satirist, a comic essayist and cartoonist, and a great novelist. If anything, they could represent the diversity of modern literature. Yet one thing unites them. They share a common idea of good style, an idea of the virtures of clarity and simplicity. This attitude toward style was not unknown to earlier writers, but never before has it been so pervasive and so exclusive.

Style is the manner of a sentence, not its matter. But the distinction between manner and matter is a slippery one, for manner affects matter. When *Time* used to tell us that President Truman slouched into one room, while General Eisenhower strode into another, their manner was trying to prejudice our feelings. The hotel that invites me to en-

---

*1980: This essay introduced an anthology of modern pronouncements on prose style, called *The Modern Stylists* (The Free Press, 1968).

joy my favorite beverage at the Crown Room is trying not to sound crass: "Have a drink at the bar." One linguist, in discussing this problem, took Caesar's "I came; I saw; I conquered," and revised it as "I arrived on the scene of the battle; I observed the situation; I won the victory." Here, the matter is the same, but Caesar's tone of arrogant dignity disappears in the pallid pedantry of the longer version. It is impossible to say that the matter is unaffected. But, let us say that this kind of difference, in the two versions of Caesar, is what we mean by style.

In the expression "good writing" or "good style," the word "good" has usually meant "beautiful" or "proficient" — like a good Rembrandt or a good kind of soap. In our time it has come to mean honest as opposed to fake. Bad writing happens when the writer lies to himself, to others, or to both. Probably, it is necessary to lie to oneself in order to lie to others; advertising men use the products they praise. Bad writing may be proficient; it may persuade us to buy a poor car or vote for an imbecile, but it is bad because it is tricky, false in its enthusiasm, and falsely motivated. It appeals to a part of us that wants to deceive itself. I am encouraged to tell myself that I am enjoying my favorite beverage when, really, I am only getting sloshed.

"If a man writes clearly enough any one can see if he fakes," says Hemingway. Orwell reverses the terms: "The great enemy of clear language is insincerity . . . . When there is a gap between one's real and one's declared aims, one turns as it were instinctively to long words and exhausted idioms, like a cuttlefish squirting out ink." Pound talks about the "gap between one's real and one's declared aims" as the distance between expression and meaning. In "The New Vocabularianism," Thurber speaks of the political use of cliches to hide a "menacing Alice in Wonderland meaninglessness." As Robert Graves says, "The writing of good English is thus a moral matter." And the morality is a morality of truth-telling. Herbert Read declares that "the only thing that is indispensable for the possession of a good style is personal sincerity." We can agree, but we must add that personal sincerity is not always an easy matter, nor is it always available to the will. Real aims, we must understand, are not necessarily conscious ones. The worst liars in the world may consider themselves sincere. Analysis of one's own style, in fact, can be a test of one's own feelings. And certainly, many habits of bad style are bad habits of thinking as well as of feeling.

There are examples of the modern attitude toward style in older writers. Jonathan Swift, maybe the best prose writer of the language, sounds like George Orwell when he writes:

. . . Our English tongue is too little cultivated in this kingdom, yet the faults are nine in ten owing to affectation, not to want of understanding. When a man's thoughts are clear, the properest words will generally offer themselves first, and his own judgment will direct him in what order to place them, so as they may be best understood.

Here Swift appears tautological; clear thoughts only *exist* when they are embodied in clear words. But he goes on: "When men err against this method, it is usually on purpose" — purposes, we must add, that we often disguise from ourselves.

Aristotle in his *Rhetoric* makes a case for plainness and

truth-telling. "The right thing in speaking really is that we should be satisfied not to annoy our hearers, without trying to delight them: we ought in fairness to fight our case with no help beyond the bare facts." And he anticipates the modern stylist's avoidance of unusual words: "Clearness is secured by using the words . . . that are current and ordinary." Cicero attacks the Sophists because they are "on the lookout for ideas that are neatly put rather than reasonable . . . ."

Yet, when we quote Cicero, the master rhetorician, on behalf of honest clarity, we must remember that the ancients did not really think of style as we do. Style until recent times has been a division of rhetoric. To learn style, one learned the types of figures of speech and the appropriateness of each to different levels of discourse — high, middle, and low. The study of style was complex, but it was technical rather than moral. For some writers, Latin was high and the vernacular low, but in the Renaissance the vernacular took in all levels. It is only in modern times that style divorces itself from rhetoric — rhetoric belongs to the enemy, to the advertisers and the propagandists — and becomes a matter of ethics and introspection.

Ezra Pound, like some French writers before him, makes the writer's function social. "Good writers are those who keep the language efficient. That is to say, keep it accurate, keep it clear." We must ask why this idea of the function of good style is so predominantly a modern phenomenon. Pound elsewhere speaks of the "assault," by which he means the attack upon our ears and eyes of words used dishonestly to persuade us, to convince us to buy or to believe. Never before have men been exposed to so many words — written words, from newspapers and billboards and paperbacks and flashing signs and the sides of buses, and spoken words, from radio and television and loudspeakers. Everyone who wishes to keep his mind clear and his feelings his own must make an effort to brush away these words like cobwebs from the face. The assault of the phoney is a result of technology combined with a morality that excuses any technique which is useful for persuasion. The persuasion is for purposes of making money, as in advertising, or winning power, as in war propaganda and the slogans of politicians. Politicians have always had slogans, but they never before had the means to spread their words so widely. The cold war of rhetoric between communism and capitalism has killed no soldiers, but the air is full of the small corpses of words that were once alive: "democracy," "freedom," "liberation."

It is because of this assault, primarily, that writers have become increasingly concerned with the honesty of their style to the exclusion of other qualities. Concentration on honesty is the only way to exclude the sounds of the bad style that assault us all. These writers are concerned finally *to be honest about what they see, feel and know.* For some of them, like William Carlos Williams, we can trust only the evidence of our eyes and ears, our real knowledge of our immediate environment.

Our reading of good writers and our attempt to write like them can help to guard us against the dulling onslaught. But we can only do this if we are able to look into ourselves with some honesty. An ethic of clarity demands intelligence and self-knowledge. Really, the ethic is not only a defense against the assault (nothing good is ever merely defensive), but is a development of the same inwardness that is reflected in psychoanalysis. One cannot, after all, examine one's motives and feelings carefully if one takes a naive view that the appearance of a feeling is the reality of that feeling.

Sometimes, the assault is merely pompous. Some people say "wealthy" instead of "rich" in order to seem proper, or "home" instead of "house" in order to seem genteel. George Orwell translates a portion of *Ecclesiastes* into academic-pompous, for example; Quiller-Couch does something similar with Hamlet's soliloquy. Years ago, James Russell Lowell ridiculed the newspapers that translated "A great crowd came to see . . ." into "A vast concourse was assembled to witness . . ." None of these examples is so funny as a colonel's statement on television that one of our astronauts "has established visual contact" with a piece of equipment. He meant that the astronaut had *seen* it.

Comic as these pompousities are, they are signs that something has gone wrong somewhere. (My father normally spoke a perfectly good plain English, but, occasionally, when he was unhappy with himself, he would fall off dreadfully; I can remember him once admonishing me at dinner, "It is necessary to masticate thoroughly.") The colonel must have been worried about the intellectual respectability of the space program when he resorted to phrases like "visual contact." The lady who speaks of "luncheon" instead of "lunch" is worried about her social status. She gives herself away. Something has gone wrong, and it has gone wrong inside her mind and her emotions.

The style is the man. Again and again, the modern stylists repeat this idea. By a man's metaphors you shall know him. When a commencement orator advises students to enrich themselves culturally, chances are that he is more interested in money than in poetry. When a university president says that his institution turned out 1,432 B.A.'s last year, he tells us that he thinks he is running General Motors. The style is the man. Remy de Gourmont used the analogy that the bird's song is conditioned by the shape of the beak. And Paul Valery said, ". . . what makes the style is not merely the mind applied to a particular action; it is the whole of a living system extended, imprinted and recognizable in expression." These statements are fine, but they sound too deterministic, as if one expresses an unalterable self and can no more change the style of that self than a bird can change the shape of its beak. Man is a kind of bird that can change his beak.

A writer of bad prose, to become a writer of good prose, must alter his character. He does not have to become good in terms of conventional morality, but he must become honest in the expression of himself, which means that he must know himself. There must be no gap between expression and meaning, between real and declared aims. For some people, some of the time, this simply means *not* telling deliberate lies. For most people, it means learning when they are lying and when they are not. It means learning the real names of their feelings. It means not saying or thinking, "I didn't *mean* to hurt your feelings," when there really existed a desire to hurt. It means not saying "luncheon" or "home" for the purpose of appearing upper-class or well-educated. It means not using the passive mood to attribute to no one in particular opinions that one is unwilling to call one's own. It means not disguising banal thinking by polysyllabic writing or the lack of feeling by clichés that purport to display feeling.

The style is the man, and the man can change himself by changing his style. Prose style is the way you think and the way you understand what you feel. Frequently, we feel for one another a mixture of strong love and strong hate; if we call it love and disguise the hate to ourselves by sentimentalizing over love, we are thinking and feeling badly. Style is ethics and psychology; clarity is a psychological sort of ethic, since it involves not general moral laws, but truth to the individual self. The scrutiny of style is a moral and psychological study. By trying to scrutinize our own style, perhaps with the help of people like Orwell and Pound, Hemingway and Thurber, we try to understand ourselves. Editing our own writing, or going over in memory our own spoken words, or even inwardly examining our thought, we can ask *why* we resorted to the passive in this case or to clichés in that. When the smoke of bad prose fills the air, something is always on fire somewhere. If the style is really the man, the style becomes an instrument for discovering and changing the man. Language is expression of self, but language is also the instrument by which to know that self.

Four Kinds Of Reading (1968)*

E VERYWHERE one meets the idea that reading is an
activity desirable in itself. It is understandable that
publishers and librarians — and even writers — should
promote this assumption, but is strange that the idea
should have general currency. People surround the idea of
reading with piety, and do not take into account the purpose of reading or the value of what is being read.
Teachers and parents praise the child who reads, and
praise themselves, whether the text be *The Reader's
Digest* or *Moby Dick*. The advent of TV has increased the
false values ascribed to reading, since TV provides a
vulgar alternative. But this piety is silly; and most reading
is no more cultural nor intellectual nor imaginative than
shooting pool or watching *What's My Line.*

It is worth asking how the act of reading became
something to value in itself, as opposed for instance to the
act of conversation or the act of taking a walk. Mass
literacy is a recent phenomenon, and I suggest that the
aura which decorates reading is a relic of the importance
of reading to our great-great-grandparents. Literacy used

to be a mark of social distinction, separating a small portion of humanity from the rest. The farm laborer who was ambitious for his children did not daydream that they would become schoolteachers or doctors; he daydreamed that they would learn to read, and that a world would therefore open up to them in which they did not have to labor in the fields fourteen hours a day for six days a week in order to buy salt and cotton. On the next rank of society, ample time for reading meant that the reader was free from the necessity to spend most of his waking hours making a living. This sort of attitude shades into the contemporary man's boast of his wife's cultural activities. When he says that his wife is interested in books and music and pictures, he is not only enclosing the arts in a female world, he is saying that he is rich enough to provide her with the leisure to do nothing. Reading is an inactivity, and therefore a badge of social class. Of course, these reasons for the piety attached to reading are never acknowledged. They show themselves in the shape of our attitudes toward books; reading gives off an air of gentility.

It seems to me possible to name four kinds of reading, each with a characteristic manner and purpose. The first is reading for information — reading to learn about a trade, or politics, or how to accomplish something. We read a newspaper this way, or most textbooks, or directions on how to assemble a bicycle. With most of this material, the reader can learn to scan the page quickly, coming up with what he needs and ignoring what is irrelevant to him, like the rhythm of the sentence, or the play of metaphor. Courses in speed reading can help us read for this purpose, training the eye to jump quickly across the page. If we read the *New York Times* with the attention we should give a novel or a poem, we will have time for nothing else, and our mind will be cluttered with clichés and dead metaphor. Quick eye-reading is a necessity to anyone who wants to keep up with what's happening, or learn much of what has happened in the past. The amount of reflection, which interrupts and slows down the reading, depends on the material.

But it is not the same activity as reading literature. There ought to be another word. If we read a work of literature properly, we read slowly, and we *hear* all the words. If our lips do not actually move, it's only laziness. The muscles in our throat move, and come together when we see the word "squeeze." We hear the sounds so accurately that if a syllable is missing in a line of poetry we hear the lack, though we may not know what we are lacking. In prose we accept the rhythms, and hear the adjacent sounds. We also register a track of feeling through the metaphors and associations of words. Careless writing prevents this sort of attention, and becomes offensive. But the great writers reward it. Only by the full exercise of our powers to receive language can we absorb their intelligence and their imagination. This kind of reading goes through the ear — though the eye takes in the print, and decodes it into sound — to the throat and the understanding, and it can never be quick. It is slow and sensual, a deep pleasure that begins with touch and ends with the sort of comprehension that we associate with dream.

Too many intellectuals read in order to reduce images to abstractions. One reads philosophy slowly, as if it were literature, but much time must be spent with the eyes turned away from the page, reflecting on the text. To read literature this way is to turn it into something it is not — to concepts clothed in character, or philosophy sugar-coated.

I think that most literary intellectuals read this way, including brighter Professors of English, with the result that
they miss literature completely, and concern themselves
with a minor discipline called the history of ideas. I
remember a course in Chaucer at my University in which
the final exam required the identification of a hundred or
more fragments of Chaucer, none as long as a line. If you
liked poetry, and read Chaucer through a couple of times
slowly, you found yourself knowing them all. If you were
a literary intellectual, well-informed about the great chain
of being, chances are you had a difficult time. To read
literature is to be intimately involved with the words on
the page, and never to think of them as the embodiments
of ideas which can be expressed in other terms. On the
other hand, intellectual writing — closer to mathematics
on a continuum that has at its opposite pole lyric poetry —
requires intellectual reading, which is slow because it is
reflective and because the reader must pause to evaluate
concepts.

But most of the reading which is praised for itself is
neither literary nor intellectual. It is narcotic. Novels,
stories, and biographies — historical sagas, monthly
regurgitations of book clubs, four- and five-thousand
word daydreams of the magazines — these are the opium
of the suburbs. The drug is not harmful except to the ad-
dict himself, and is no more injurious to him than Johnny
Carson or a bridge club, but it is nothing to be proud of.
This reading is the automated daydream, the mild trip of
the housewife and the tired businessman, interested not in
experience and feeling but in turning off the possibilities
of experience and feeling. Great literature, if we read it
well, opens us up to the world, and makes us more sensitive to it, as if we acquired eyes that could see through

walls and ears that could hear the smallest sounds. But by narcotic reading, one can reduce great literature to the level of *The Valley of the Dolls*. One can read *Anna Karenina* passively and inattentively, and float down the river of lethargy as if one were reading a confession magazine: "I Spurned My Husband for a Count."

I think that everyone reads for narcosis occasionally, and perhaps most consistently in late adolescence, when great readers are born. I remember reading to shut the world out, away at a school where I did not want to be; I invented a word for my disease: "bibliolepsy," on the analogy of narcolepsy. But after a while the books became a window on the world, and not a screen against it. This change doesn't always happen. I think that late adolescent narcotic reading accounts for some of the badness of English departments. As a college student, the boy loves reading and majors in English because he would be reading anyway. Deciding on a career, he takes up English teaching for the same reason. Then in graduate school he is trained to be a scholar, which is painful and irrelevant, and finds he must write papers and publish them to be a Professor — and at about this time he no longer requires reading for narcosis, and he is left with nothing but a Ph.D. and the prospect of fifty years of teaching literature; and he does not even like literature.

Narcotic reading survives the impact of television, because this type of reading has even less reality than melodrama; that is, the reader is in control: once the characters reach into the reader's feelings, he is able to stop reading, or glance away, or superimpose his own daydream. The trouble with television is that it embodies its own daydream. Literature is often valued precisely because of its distance from the tangible. Some readers prefer looking into the text of a play to seeing it performed. Reading a play, it is possible to stage it oneself by an imaginative act; but it is also possible to remove it from real people. Here is Virginia Woolf, who was lavish in her praise of the act of reading, talking about reading a play rather than seeing it: "Certainly there is a good deal to be said for reading *Twelfth Night* in the book if the book can be read in a garden, with no sound but the thud of an apple falling to the earth, or of the wind ruffling the branches of the trees." She sets her own stage; the play is called *Virginia Woolf Reads Twelfth Night in a Garden.* Piety moves into narcissism, and the high metaphors of Shakespeare's lines dwindle into the flowers of an English garden; actors in ruffles wither, while the wind ruffles branches.

Poets On The Platform (1966)

WHEN I was young, it was a well-known fact that the Poet had lost touch with his Audience. Every December, in its annual literary review, *Time* lamented this loss, as if *Time* wanted nothing so much as a book of poems to read in the club car. Later I noticed the crocodile behind the tears (the one unbeatable way to hate poetry is to praise poetry two generations back), and I realized that the golden age of Poet and Audience was fantasy. Martin Tupper outsold Tennyson; Edgar Guest outsold Robert Frost. Yet in a sense that *Time* never intended, its prayers are answered. The American poet, who twenty years ago lacked an audience, has one today. This audience is not metaphorical: it is row upon row of college students, mixed with a few professors and the old people who gather in college towns. The lecture-platform is revolutionizing the life of the American poet and probably his poetry as well.

Sometimes the poet reads his own poems, sometimes he lectures, often he visits classes, always he makes contact with the young, formally and informally, from the lectern and over the coffee-cup. Sometimes he visits one campus a day on a circuit that keeps him moving for a week or two. Sometimes he spends two days or a week at a particular institution. Ten years ago lecture agents handled only the most prominent poets; now they take on the younger and less-known, if they are good performers.

Lots of poets are mimics and ham actors anyway — they enjoy doing imitations of W. C. Fields and James Cagney at a late stage of the party — and in any case the increasing importance of the platform in the poet's life leads him to learn to perform. There are a few who hate and avoid the platform, but they are a minority. For me, it is an old wish come true. When I was at an age when anything seemed possible — thirteen or fourteen perhaps — I hesitated between becoming a great actor or a great poet. Poetry won the struggle over my soul, but now because I am a poet I am permitted to be an actor. I thrive on the theatre of it all.

I pace up and down in the green room before I come on stage, being sure to make myself nervous if I am not nervous enough to begin with. I walk to the lectern under the applause, smiling and feeling wretched, and within a minute I am swollen (like Mr. Toad) with the delights of control and ease: *I hold them in my hand.* I have learned tricks that can keep a convocation from coughing and wriggling. (A convocation can be described as an enforced gathering of 600 youths of whom 594 have never read a poem voluntarily.)

Because of the increasing popularity of the platform, poets are beginning to be able to support themselves as poets, not as teachers or vicars or advertising men. The economics of poetry is more peculiar than ever: if the poet publishes forty poems in a range of magazines, he may gross as much as $600; when he collects these poems into a book, the royalties after a few years are likely to be about $600 also. But for reading the same poems for one hour at a college, the poet may receive $750 or $1,000, and he can do thirty or forty lectures a year. To complete the anomaly, the same college is often too poor — in its library allocation — to own his books.

So the lecture-platform can provide the poet his income. Also, it helps the American poet to keep in touch with other poets in this huge country; the Midwesterner with a reading in New Jersey can spend a day in New York at the Eighth Street Bookstore and among his New York friends. Perhaps most valuable, there is the contact with those who are not friends — conversations in classes and question periods and coffee hours.

Last year in Massachusetts I had just finished reading to a convocation when a young man came up to me. He was obviously in a great hurry to get somewhere, and had time only to ask one important question. "Who's the better poet," he asked, "Gibran or Dylan?" I was startled. "Gibran is rubbish," I said. "Dylan Thomas is a great poet." He looked surprised. "I don't mean Dylan *Thomas*," he said. It was from him that I learned about Bob Dylan's vogue as a poet, and went out therefore and read him, and decided that his poetry was rubbish too.

But one learns not only about fads. At nearly every college there is someone, a student or a teacher, who becomes for the moment important. Either you have said something useful to someone, or you find that you have learned something yourself. There can be many *kinds* of learning. Reading a poem is a form of publication, an objectification that can show the poet something he had not seen before. When I get to a certain stage in writing a poem — when I can't see anything wrong with it, but I sense that it is not finished — I read it aloud to my Audience. Often I know instantly, as I read it, where the fault is. Without the reality of those faces, the poem would not have been changed as it was.

The reality of those faces is bound to change the kind of poetry Americans write. The poet's removal from the classroom to the platform, his traveling, his public identity as an artist — all these things will touch his poems. Some of the changes could be bad. Suppose a poet were led to write only poems which could be grasped at a single hearing. The consequent limits on style and subject matter would be debilitating: there are a good number of Shakespeare's poems, and Robert Frost's, which are too obscure to pass such a test.

In the past I've written some poems that were more directed toward the ear, and some that were more directed toward the eye. The latter were usually in syllabics, and were essayistic in tone, like this passage from a poem called "An American in an Essex Village," from my last book*:

Yet inside the Church, he remembers,
  the death-watch beetle hollows
    six-hundred-year-old
  beams. The Vicar reconstructs
old music and Sarum liturgy
    for twelve souls.

I no longer want to write this sort of poem because it does not read well aloud. It's hard to make it happen with your

---

*A Roof of Tiger Lilies, 1963.

voice; the audience stirs, the eyes wander.

Instead, I want to write poems in which the sound itself keeps the listeners intent, like (as I hope) a tiny poem called "Reclining Figure":

Then the knee of the wave
turned to stone.

By the cliff of her flank
I anchored,

in the darkness of harbors
laid-by.

Listeners don't have to understand this poem intellectually, but to enjoy it as a sensual object, to take it into their ears and be moved by it, whether they know what I'm talking about or not.

The problem arises of the boundaries between writing and performance. Poets like me, who find performing nearly as attractive as writing, are in danger of becoming not poets but scriptwriters for our own one-man shows. If all poems are written for the voice of the poet, our poetry will become increasingly oral, which sounds like a good thing. But the good poem must exist on the page as well as on the platform, and there is the danger that actor-poets will sacrifice the poetry to the performance.

A little while ago I was working on the draft of a poem and was troubled by a particular phrase. It wasn't accurate enough; there were too many irrelevant associations, instead of the precision I looked for. "But anyway" — I caught myself thinking, as I failed to cross it out — "I can *say* it so they'll know what I mean."

Metallic Flowers (1966)*

A FEW YEARS ago I noticed that Wordsworth's poem "The Daffodils" was about economics. The surface, or plot, of the poem says that the poet takes a walk, sees a field of daffodils, and that his pleasure endures. Here are the first three stanzas of the poem:

> I wandered lonely as a cloud
> That floats on high o'er vales and hills,
> When all at once I saw a crowd,
> A host, of golden daffodils,
> Beside the lake, beneath the trees
> Fluttering and dancing in the breeze
>
> Continuous as the stars that shine
> And twinkle on the Milky Way,
> They stretched in never-ending line
> Along the margin of a bay:

---

*Adapted from an article in the *New York Times Book Review* and from *The Pleasures of Poetry*, Harper & Row, 1971.

Ten thousand saw I at a glance
Tossing their heads in sprightly dance.

The waves beside them danced, but they
Outdid the sparkling waves in glee:
A poet could not but be gay
In such a jocund company!
I gazed — and gazed — but little thought
What wealth the show to me had brought

The poem is, of course, about daffodils, and shows a joy in the flowers which is surely genuine. Yet there is another side to the poem, which exists in the words and can be derived from the words by close attention, and which belongs to a world entirely different from the world of nature and daffodils.

For many years I read the poem with pleasure, but with a dim sense that something was happening in it which I did not understand. Finally I took a closer look at it. Really, Wordsworth is rather odd about these daffodils. Indeed he emphasizes the pleasure they gave him. But in describing the flowers themselves, he does two unusual things. First, he does not talk about a single daffodil, which one might want to isolate and contemplate; rather, he emphasizes the *quantity* of the daffodils. Even before we have the name of the flower, we have "a crowd,/A host." Then the imagery multiplies them: "Continuous as the stars . . . on the Milky Way" and ". . . never-ending line," and finally he names a falsely specific large number. (False specificity is a common tradition of lively speech and of poetry.) "Ten thousand."

Second, Wordsworth talks in a *peculiar* way about the color of the flowers. Daffodils are yellow, indeed, and in his first reference to the daffodils Wordsworth uses the alternative word, "golden." It is a perfectly fine word, but there is no such thing as a synonym, and there are various ways in which "yellow" and "golden" differ. Some of the differences are trivial, perhaps, but some are certainly not. The difference that Wordsworth chooses to exploit is the metallic overtone in "golden" — an overtone which is an intimation of riches. Words like "shine" and "twinkle" would not seem normally appropriate to daffodils. (Those numerous stars have intervened; but what applies to stars must apply to daffodils as well.)

"Shine" and "twinkle" work in this poem because of the metallic connotation of "golden." "Sparkling" continues the image, and then Wordsworth ends the third stanza with extraordinary skill by bringing together in one metaphor his two themes of quantity and gold. What happens if you have a lot of this metal? You're rich, that's what happens. "I gazed — and gazed — but little thought/What wealth the show to me had brought." Wordsworth makes inescapable his comparison: Looking at the daffodils was like suddenly inheriting a great deal of money. It takes great skill to combine two different lines of imagery, two remote metaphorical areas (one of color, and one of quantity) and to bring them together in a single word, so that they are welded together inescapably. The word "weatlth" performs just this act of skill. I am virtually certain that Wordsworth was unaware of his economic metaphor; therefore, we have an example of superb technical skill which is unconscious.

Wordsworth carries the comparison further. He asks himself, "What does a sensible person do when he suddenly acquires a great deal of money?" and he answers, "He invests it, and lives on the income." Look at the fourth and final stanza of the poem:

For oft, when on my couch I lie
In vacant or in pensive mood,
They flash upon that inward eye
Which is the bliss of solitude;
And then my heart with pleasure fills,
And dances with the daffodils.

Let me set an arithmetic problem: Ten-thousand daffodils at six percent is how many daydreams a year?

Ever since I noticed this covert meaning to the poem — that it is about money at least as much as it is about flowers — I have delighted in telling people about it, and I once described it in an article. Some people think I am joking, possibly satirizing a sort of criticism, and many others are outraged at what they consider a sacrilege. I *do* think that the disparity between the two levels of the poem is comical, but I am not making a joke. (If I were interested in trying to be funny, I could assert that "the margin of a bay" was a reference to buying on the margin.) I truly believe that this meaning exists in the poem as a result of the unconscious intention of the poet. Far from ruining the poem, this further level increases its fascination. The first few times we read the poem with covert meaning in mind, the comic disparity may split our vision a trifle, but eventually we can hold both meanings in mind at once, and appreciate the poem as the complicated act of a human psyche.

Unconscious intentions are common to good poetry. T.S. Eliot said somewhere that the meaning of a poem is always only ostensible. If the poem lives, there is a content that was hidden from the poet at the time he wrote. If I write a poem about X, and someone later points out to me that it is really about Y, I am pleased: only an un-acknowledged power can make the engine go: only the mysterious *works*.

Unconscious content is unconscious for strong reasons, because we do not wish to acknowledge it. Here Wordsworth writes a poem in praise of money and invest-ment. Wordsworth's England was Marx's England, the England of child labor and the slums of Manchester. Wordsworth turned his back on the slums, the child labor, and the factories. They were ugly and nasty, and he could not bear to see them. He could look at London only before the day's work had started.

But there is a strange justice in the psyche: If you live in the country to forget that your prosperity derives from exploitation, you will look at flowers and praise them in terms of money. I remember the anecdote that gave John O'Hara the title of a novel: The old Sultan, noticing the figure of Death lurking in his courtyard, hurriedly de-parts for Samara to hide from him. Another person seeing Death stops for a chat, but Death says he has no time to talk; he has an appointment in Samara.

Anyone who feels that his appreciation of the poem is harmed by this reading never appreciated it in the first place; he is thinking only of some picture postcard of the English countryside which a teacher substituted for the poem. Postcards are easier to handle than poems, which are as complicated as people. If we read the poem openly, it seems to me, the daffodils are still there, and the im-agination that walks among them dreams of them later. But the imagination is specifically capitalist, not feudal or socialist, and as the daffodils move in the breeze and touch each other, they make a clinking sound.

When I published some of these paragraphs in the *New York Times Book Review*, I received a deluge of letters from outraged Wordsworthians. One lady told me that the only clinking sound was in my head. Another letter made me realize that unconscious intentions exist in literary articles too, and not just in poems — or that they probably do; I will never know for sure. When I was about sixteen I had an English teacher with whom I had a great quarrel. A few days after my article had been published, I received a letter from him enclosing a postcard of daffodils in the lake country. He said that my fingerprints were still on the card. I did not remember, and still do not, that he handed the postcard around in my class. But I have a strong suspicion that he did, and that some part of me knew it, and that my phrase, "some picture postcard ... which a teacher substituted for the poem," which I thought I just made up, was really a piece of long-term revenge.

The Inward Muse (1965)*

I AM ASKED to talk about the critic *in* the poet, or the function of the critical intelligence in the creative process. Therefore I must give an account of the creative process as a whole. Since no one has ever defined the creative process convincingly, I have a lot to accomplish in a short space.

To investigate the process of writing poems, one can go to a number of sources for ideas and information; one can go to literary history and learn about the habits and manuscripts of great authors. One can go to literary theory and discover the illogic of some of our presuppositions. One can go to the huge literature about creativity which is emerging from psychology, especially psychoanalytical psychology. (Most of my reading in the last few months has been in this third area, and I will try to make use — in an eclectic and unscientific way — of what I have learned.) But I suspect that a fourth source has deter-

*1980: This essay was delivered as a lecture at the University of Iowa in 1965, part of a symposium on "The Poet as Critic."

mined my choices among the data supplied by the other three, and has picked what fits and ignored what doesn't fit; the fourth source is introspection, memory, scrutiny of my own experience of making poems.

Even to talk about the critical intelligence in the creative process is to suggest a possible mistake, because it implies a separation between two types of thinking which is rarely discernible in practice. Almost all writing about the creative process, whether by poets or critics or psychoanalysts, has involved a theoretical dualism of *creation* which provides material, and *criticism* which shapes it. When Eliot wrote that "The critical activity finds its highest truest fulfillment in a *kind of union* with creation in the labour of the artist" (my italics), he was writing the epigraph for my contribution to the subject of "the poet as critic." More typical is Edmund Bergler's separation of the process into two *phases*, as if they occurred in sequence. The first phase is the release of material from the id, distorted indeed — a system of drives, defenses and counterdefenses. Then, "The second phase consists of work, often hard work, to form and develop the material received from unconscious sources; experience, tact, great technical skill are needed in this phase." How neat and orderly we are. Buried in this scheme is an economic metaphor of raw material, factory and consumer. Dr. Bergler ignores the psychological meaning of "technical skill" — a cliche as he uses it — and concentrates only on drives and defenses. He also displays an unacknowledged puritanism: after the orgy of the id, there is the hard work of the consciousness. This dualism conjures up fantastic scenes: from a dim swamp there emerges the hulking green monster of the id, its jaws drooling blood as it looks for another child to eat, then, separate, appears the critical

116

intelligence, cheerful, walking in the bright sun, wearing sensible shoes, a clean little professor with an umbrella. When he encounters the monster he *works hard* on him, reforms him, and — presto! — the monster becomes John V. Lindsay, both disciplined and handsome.

The responsibility for many of the misleading ideas about the creative process belongs to poets. Poets tend to represent themselves either as detached craftsmen or as inspired, unconscious, mad mouthpieces. Poe is the ultimate craftsman, at least in his pose. One may not accept that the outside — the pose — represents what really happens inside, but poses are serious; as Pasternak said, you need the pose before you can have the poem. Poe tells us that he planned "The Raven" formally before he thought of the content, that he arrived at the subject, the death of a beautiful woman, rationally; perhaps indeed this was the way it seemed to him. In another context, T.S. Eliot wrote, "One might even hazard the conjecture that the care for perfection of form, among some of the romantic poets of the nineteenth century, was an effort to support, or to conceal from view, an inner disorder." Poe *had* to write necrophilia; therefore in order to write at all his consciousness had to deny his obsession. He could only write "The Raven" if he treated it like a crossword puzzle. Oscar Wilde has Gilbert say, in *The Critic as Artist*, "All fine imaginative work is self-conscious and deliberate. No poet sings because he must sing." Here we must understand that the author of *The Picture of Dorian Gray* is concealing from himself the emotional necessity of his work.

The pose of being detached from the content, or of being interested only in technique, is what allows the forbidden content to happen. I remember talking to W.D. Snodgrass once about some new techniques that each of us were trying out — something utterly complicated and probably, from the point of view of the reader, pointless — like a syllabic stanza of eighty-seven syllables in which every thirteenth word began with *w*. And Mr. Snodgrass said that the reason we concentrate so much on technique is that this absorption of the consciousness may allow a previously censored content to seep up onto the page. With awareness of psychoanalytical theory, one becomes conscious of the possibilities of stimulating parts of one's psyche. The technique of removing or absorbing the surface of the mind is an old one. Gertrude Stein used to write in a car parked at a Paris intersection — all those horns beeping, and Hart Crane on occasion wrote drinking wine and playing Ravel's "Bolero" over and over again. Northrop Frye says somewhere that "It takes a great deal of will-power to write poetry, but some of the will must be used to relax the will." Here the use of the same word for two things helps to relieve us of the fallacy of a division between critical and creative.

Some poets use technique to absorb the will; others use alcohol to relax it. Really — though they look utterly different — they are doing the same thing. They are out-maneuvering the restrictiveness and timidity of the conscious mind. I am proposing a unitary view of the creative process. I wish to suggest that the poets who give divergent accounts of their own processes are *using* their accounts in order to move toward a center. Even the convention among Greek poets of being mad, as Plato reports it, was a pose that could stimulate the removal of conscious barriers. I do not believe that Blake really hallucinated voices; those voices came back and dictated revisions. For that matter, I don't believe that "Kubla Khan" was a dream-poem. I think one must be skeptical of all extreme accounts of process. Whenever I hear a poet talking manic possession, I hear a man possessed by a self-protective consciousness, who is looking for a way out.

A poem happens when different aspects of the mind manage to *coincide*. Keats said, "My judgment is as active when I am writing as my imagination." There they are again, under different names, the two sides. But judgment and imagination coincided in the same actions, made "a kind of union." To write (or to cross out) a word was simultaneously an act of judgment and of imagination, of the critic and of the creator. There are, of course, different moments in the process of writing a poem. Often a poem will start with wild excitement and finish some months later with slow consideration. There is the story of Shelley observed scribbling a poem in haste, and then telling his observer, "In the morning, when cooled down, out of the rude sketch . . . I shall attempt a drawing." The drawing is as imaginative and as creative as the sketch; new words must be found, new decisions made; imagination and judgment must continue to coincide. Often in the long process of writing a poem there will be a second or a third moment of wild excitement followed by slow consideration.

One of the fascinating phenomena in dealing with a mental event is the way in which the same technique can be used for opposite purposes. Take rhyme for example. A conventional defense of rhyme — I remember Howard Nemerov speaking of it somewhere — is that it gives the poet ideas, stimulates his imagination, by suggesting (through the search for new sounds) words, ideas, symbols, and metaphors which would otherwise not have occurred to him. Rhyme is a kind of creative accident, more controlled than paint-splashing, but largely fortuitous. On the other hand, Dryden praised rhyme for a reason that must seem almost opposite; he preferred rhyme to blank verse because it *curbed* his fancy, held him down, kept him from going on and on. Really, both statements could be made by the same poet. But the fact that one poet emphasizes rhyme as an opener-up, and another, rhyme as a closer-down, reveals that each poet is seeking to complete himself; each poet is searching for the unification of imagination and choice.

Bad poetry is a result of defective creative process, which is a result of neurosis (the inability to unify the psychic components of creativity may be caused by anxiety over regression, for instance). Sometimes there is a discernible imbalance in the just-bad poem, but since poetry is a unity, an imbalance usually causes everything to be wrong. Any poetry editor will tell you that most of what he sees is unrevised garbage, slewed out verses in which there is no attempt at significant order. Yet, if one said that it was merely lacking in technical skill, one would imply that there was an appreciable content to which there was applied insufficient talent or technical experience. This is aesthetically invalid, psychologically invalid — and invisible in the text. One doesn't discern great emotions undisciplined by form — horses without reins — because such things are not discernible in poetry. A mute inglorious "Lycidas" is as unlikely as a mute inglorious Milton. Likewise, the contrary fault, which fills the literary magazines, is not small emotions overcontrolled. That's impossible too. A tiny subject, or not very moving poem, can be boring perhaps, but it's more likely to be satisfying if the form is precise, finished, whole. What we abhor is the poem in which the language and form have the rhetoric, the roll and sweep of great emotions, which are not made actual or present in the poem. This is the case of the reins without the horse, or more accurately, the reins faking the horse.

The creative process is at fault when a poem fails — but that's tautology, because you can tell the process fails only when the poem fails. But we have asserted healthy creative process as the simultaneity of complementary qualities in the act of writing. It is time to become more empirical and to observe as much as possible of this process in which judgment and imagination are one. Frank Barron speaks of "an incessant dialectic between integration and diffusion," and Marion Milner talks of an oscillation between the "oceanic state" (in *Civilization and its Discontents*, Freud described the oceanic feeling: that diffuse sense of belonging to all and being sensitive to all, which Freud relates to the baby's sense of oneness with the breast and indeed the rest of the universe) and the surface mind. Now I don't believe that it is the surface mind which is usually in question, as I will make clear in a moment, but I do think that there *is* an oscillation so rapid as hardly to seem to occupy time, between a diffuse attentive expectancy, into which words or phrases float, and another observing part of the mind which takes note and measures. I do not mean simply to give new names to the old creative-critical split, however. The two ends of the oscillation both include imagining and judging. The depth mind to which we pay diffused attention does not simply supply unjudged, undifferentiated material. Although I believe, for whatever it means, that a regression is involved, and that the depth mind even as we are able to glimpse it shows characteristics of the primary process like condensation and identification, the fact remains that changes and choices occur — critical actions — before the conscious intellect appears or knows what is going on at all. (I am assuming that I can call *critical* whatever discriminates, judges, and chooses — whether or not it is conscious.)

Poems begin any number of ways, but here is a frequent way. It is snowing, the first snow of the year. I become sleepy with the snow, I relax, daydream, enter that sleepy and almost hallucinating state I recognize as preluding a poem; my spirit wanders out of myself into the snow, and phrases come into my head. Suddenly I realize that snow does this to me, every year especially first snow. I must write about it in order to try to understand it. Snow is, in psychoanalytic language, overdetermined for me. It is burdened with affect, heavy with a nameless emotion. Being overdetermined, it must have multiple sources. I try to keep my attention diffuse and responsive to suggestion, my pen moving, as one thing leads to another down the page. I am trying to reach, be true to, exploit, the multiple sources of this overdetermination.

I don't take dictation from my unconscious mind. As I write, there is no question of simply putting down what I think. I think too fast, too much, to write down all of it, or even to dictate it if I had a machine by me. (It is for this reason that we cannot take seriously the policy of non-revision, advocated by so serious a man as Robert Duncan, on the assumption that the revision is false to the original form of the poem in the mind; this policy implies that the poem was, at one time, a single thing and not a horde of alternatives.) Words come into my head, flipping over like a deck of cards. Sometimes I choose, pausing a moment and having reasons; most of the time the word written down is one that presents itself saying pretty please, bowing. You know those series of choices that poets always put in the margins of their worksheets: large, small, tiny, huge, green, horrid, aimless, yellow. One of them — say "yellow" — comes into the mind wearing italics. It is overdetermined; it announces itself as already chosen. The multiple sources may include the image of the color, the associations with certain flowers, the oral pleasure of the syllables in the context, and a hundred other things — one is seldom aware of them at the time.

In a later draft, the word "yellow" may one day find itself discarded. One trusts the affect at the start, and writes the word down, knowing that the conviction of its rightness may prove to be perfectly incorrect. (The worst poems in the world have been written down with a certainty of inspired genius. So have the best.) The word which seemed so right at the start may turn out wrong because the poem changed as it developed; a poem as it grows sets its own standard, by which each component of the poem will have to be judged. Or more likely, the cathexis involved only a part of the word. One made a judgment (the word seemed to come forth already judged) forgetting something — that "yellow" in a poem about snow reminds one of dogs urinating perhaps, or that a near-rhyme with "hero" is jarring to the ear. But my point is that some form of judgment or criticism is involved in the writing down of any word, good or bad, in any draft.

There is also the shape of the poem on the page and to the ear. This takes us to the second half of our oscillating pair. There is in the mind of the poet a great deal of learned form, technique, and mastery, of which he is not immediately conscious. The preconscious has been invented to take care of this sort of thing. This formal activity takes

123

place, I think, neither in the depth mind, with its drives and defenses and counterdefenses, nor on the surface mind (*contra* Marion Milner), with its reasons and its secondary elaboration. The depth mind has no sense of gestalt, which is perhaps one reason why babies aren't great writers. The preconscious is the primary locus of the satisfaction one feels in the *wholeness* of a work of art.

One of my old teachers, when he urges his students to acquire poetic techniques, likes to talk about the training of Joe Louis who apparently began life as a prize fighter lacking in footwork. His trainers marked the gym floor with chalk to set him exercises, over and over — rather like doing heroic couplets with medial caesuras — until he had the moves by heart and did them without thinking. There is thinking in writing poetry (I suspect there is in prize fighting), but an enormous amount of our judging, deciding, choosing is made without conscious thought. A sense of poetic form becomes "second nature," as the idiom has it. The satisfaction we feel in the achieved gestalt is the click of the lid of the perfectly made box, which Yeats heard in the finished poem.

The preconscious of a poet comes from all the poems he has used and heard used, and the arguments he has had with his friends. It works, as the poem unfolds itself down the page, as a system of possibilities, like the system of the sonnet, or the system of blank verse, but infinitely more various than those superficial forms. Knowledge of sonnet form and blank verse resides in the preconscious. Anyone who has had much experience of either form has acquired a great deal of knowledge which will inform his choices without being verbalized. But in free verse as well, our preconscious has acquired, through reading and talking and thinking, ideas of what a good noise may sound like. Maybe the word "yellow" was chosen instead of the word "gold" because the cadence rejected a monosyllable at this point in the poem. If so, the preconscious was imagining and judging poetic form. "Ear" — that mysterious word which poets love — is a quality of the preconscious mainly, I think. Articulated ear, the movement of the whole poem in time, is surely preconscious. There is the other kind of ear — Dylan Thomas as opposed to Milton — which is unimpressive as a long rhythm but satisfying in the immediate pronunciation. This second kind of ear is an oral satisfaction while the longer rhythmic type is a gestalt satisfaction. Oral satisfaction, to some degree, is present in all good poems, and comes I think more from unconscious, instinctual sources — a regression to the pleasure of the infant at the breast — than from conscious or preconscious formal standards, which pertain to the ego.

In writing the poem about snow, the words seemed naturally to fall into six-line, free-verse stanzas, two or three accents a line. Six months later, I suspect, the form would have been different. Sometimes one chooses a type of line on purpose, but most often in my experience a poem seems to choose its own. However, if I think hard enough, I can usually figure out the circumstances which led to the particular line and stanza. The choice was not conscious, but it is explicable. For instance, one day I find myself thinking something like this: "I've been writing all my free verse in lines of about the same length and in stanzas; that's because I have a nostalgia for tight rhymed iambic forms; why not be brave and go in for asymmetry all the way?" Two weeks later when a poem starts to come, it presents itself as asymmetrical, though I do not will it to come so. The preconscious has absorbed my earlier conscious thought and erected it into a temporary and tentative standard.

I have been using two different ideas — unconscious overdetermination and preconscious knowledge — to talk about critical choices made when one is not being conscious. Let me talk about one more poem. In the snow poem, I was trying to understand my overresponse to a natural phenomenon. A month or two after writing about the snow, a phrase came into my head, unattached to anything natural — I have never discovered the source of it, in my reading or in conversation — simply the name of an animal, the musk-ox. And with it came a rhythm, a highly percussive and strange beat. I had no idea what it meant, but it came bearing the credentials of strong feeling and I trusted it as I have learned to do. I worked out the rhythm consciously, and over two years hammered out a short poem which has virtually no rational content. (It is a short inconsequential narrative.) By the end of the two years I began to see what, in a sense, I was talking about. To my surprise at least a few other people understood it too. In this poem the working out of the rhythm (a scheme of louds and softs irregularly spaced from line to line, but each stanza repeating the same line-structure) gave me great trouble, absorbed consciousness, allowed me to think of the poem as music or abstract painting, and so allowed the poem to explore an area of sexual feeling which I would otherwise have kept hidden from myself. In this case a consciousness of form — in the obvious sense of repeated measure — absorbed consciousness. Of course at the same time, all my years of reading and technical striving were at work preconsciously, measuring and judging the poise of syllables, the rub of a verb against a noun, the degree of an enjambment.

Most of the deciding and the criticizing, then, takes place as the hand moves; and the hand moves before the consciousness tells it to move. (There is a final nit-picking stage at which I interrogate the poem consciously, but it generally contributes little to the poem as a whole.) There is no kind of balance between conscious and unconscious in a poem, because there is so little that is fully conscious. But there is an oscillation, and even within the extremes of the oscillation — where directions from unconscious sources are deployed under the conditions of preconsciousness — there is a certain doubleness in the psyche of the poet, and in the definition of the poem.

The definition of a good poem, I have always said, requires the idea of an audience. That audience can be one person — probably *is* one person — but it is someone other than the poet. The poet, if he is a good one, has to include this critic in his own psyche. It is part of the psychic machinery that makes a poet. The Muse, I strongly suspect, is the critic-God within us, to whom all poems are truly addressed. A few years back, answering a question about the audience at which a poem is aimed, Richard Wilbur named the Muse, and said the Muse was invented to cover up the fact that the poem was addressed to nobody in particular. I agree that the Muse is the reader, but not that she is no one in particular. Superficially she is a compound of our six best friends, our wife, and Shakespeare; really, she is probably good old Mom. She is another survival of infancy, like most of the things that make a poem. When a baby has the oceanic feeling and then is deprived of his contact with the breast, he invents (believes in) an eaten-up mother, who by his fantasy lives inside him. He takes the outside world into himself, and becomes an autarchy, subject and object, creator and appreciator, eventually poet and critic. The oscillation in the creative process, so rapid as to be invisible, is between the mother giving milk (poet giving out words) and the baby drinking it (critic exercising his taste). I am aware that I have just had the critic as both mother and baby, the poet as both baby and mother; reversibility is a characteristic of the depth mind. There are pregnancy fantasies involved here too. A book is a birth, and who has not experienced that postpartum depression?

Inside this small world of the creative process, peopled by the giver and the receiver, a dialogue continues as the poem changes and becomes more and more solid or objectified or firm in its formulation. Then the dialogue moves outside or closer to outside, although always, I think, on the model of the autarchy and with reference to the autarchy. When my poems are new I cannot show them to anyone at all. The psychic balance, the necessary oscillation, would be interrupted by the presence of an exterior spirit. Three's a crowd. Later comes a moment when I seek out the opinion of friends, by letter or in person; at first only a few, then when the poem is more secure, a greater number. But there is really an intermediate step, a dialogue not with the faceless Muse that I have eaten, but with imagined friends. I don't do it on purpose, though I could, I think. It is a way of testing the poem, objectifying it a bit further, I think: What will Robert think of this? Louis? Their voices speak to me, in characteristic accents and language. Sometimes I get angry with them for their obtuseness or nastiness; at other times suddenly they say something negative and acute, that I hadn't known about the poem. My fantasy of another voice, another way of thinking, has shown me something I didn't know. The hand without being bidden crosses out a line.

I must admit that when I was younger I invented the voices of well-known elders who criticized me. Though I daydreamed sometimes of applause from Mr. Eliot and Mr. Pound — "Well done, Hall!" "By God, you've done it again!" — these daydreams were only like the eternal cables from Sweden inviting me to accept the Nobel Prize. It was not they who gave me criticism, but an editor and critic and poet who was nearly a literary dictator for a brief period, although I doubt that he aspired to such status. I grew up in the thick of the new criticism, and as I stared at my young verses I could sometimes hear the voice of Mr. Ransom, whom I had never met, intimating, "Mustuh Hall, You ah pleased to be ironical?" It took me ten years to get rid of that voice. And I have tried not merely to substitute the voice of Theodore Roethke or Charles Olson; and I cannot really enclose the Chilean voice of Pablo Neruda.

Objectifying is a series of concentric circles. First there is the oscillation between breast and baby. Then there is the imagined dialogue and the real dialogue with friends. For me, there is also a point at which it is useful to read the poem aloud at a poetry reading. One is not after comments from the crowd, but a speechless feedback. Really, it is simply an aid to the eaten-up Muse that lives inside us. (This is what I mean when I say that all objectification occurs in relation to the autarchy.) The faces listening make the poem more distant, frame it, print it. At another level of objectivity there is magazine publication. Frequently, when I compare a Robert Lowell poem, in magazine and book, I find he has revised and improved it. Then there is book publication. One reason some poets lust after selection and collection is not so much vanity as a desire to improve their poems, to alter the record.

The poet is a critic wherever he sits down to write, because he has a critic inside him. The critic — like any critic worth his salt — knows what he likes before he knows why he likes it. The critic is two things in particular: the one I have called a critic is not the usual one; he is the choice by overdetermination from the depth mind. The other is almost a traditional critic; the creation of a set of standards, changing, enlarging, narrowing as the poet ages and reads and endures, existing first of all in the preconscious but reachable by the intelligence, particularly through the use of the psychic device of internal dialogue, in the oscillation of kinds of vision. Mostly, one knows as one grows older to trust the inward Muse, to try to adjust one's psyche so that the dialogue between the parts of one's autarchy is not interrupted. We search for a receptive passivity, thinking of the poem as a creature within us, within the unimaginable complex which *is* us, but over which our consciousness has small control. Let me end my essay by quoting a small poem that I wrote several years ago, which is appropriate, I think, to these reflections. It is called:

The Poem

It discovers by night
what the day hid from it.
Sometimes it turns itself
into an animal.
In summer it takes long walks
by itself where meadows
fold back from ditches.
Once it stood still

in a quiet row of machines.
Who knows
what it is thinking?*

---

*1980: I regret the eclectic jargon of this essay. I now realize that it is possible to speak of the creative process in images and analogies which are one's own, and not borrowed with degrees of inaccuracy from a library of psychology. In *Goatfoot Milktongue Twinbird* (University of Michigan Press, 1978) there is an essay called "The Vatic Voice" which was originally appended to this essay; and the title essay of that volume is an inquiry into the psychic origins of poetic *form.* I reprint "The Inward Muse" despite my misgivings because I think its suggestions valid and not yet commonplace.

Whitman: The Invisible World (1967)*

1.

THERE IS a tiny poem that Walt Whitman wrote when he was an old man which will serve to introduce his work and his character. It is called, "These Carols":

> These carols sung to cheer my passage through the
>   world I see,
> For completion I dedicate to the Invisible World.

The familiar doubleness is here — "the world I see," and "the Invisible World" — and emphasis falls upon the latter phrase as it must. Many of Whitman's admirers, I think, consider that he chiefly concerns himself with the world he sees. They speak of his catalogues, his multiplication of *things*. Yet, the seen world hardly exists for

*1980: This essay introduced *A Choice of Whitman's Verse* (Faber, 1968) and was addressed to English readers.

132

him, because he spiritualizes everything. He is the ultimate poet of dream. When he sings of him*self*, he is removed from egotism precisely through inwardness; this self that he observes through imagination has become all selves; he *is* the multitude he called himself. The outer world, the world of jobs and brothers, is passage which songs can cheer you through, and songs, when the truth is out, are all dedicated to the Invisible World. Appearances in poetry are the colors and shapes of spirit by which Whitman brings us into his Invisible World, which he insists is also ours if we will only discover it. Like William Blake or D.H. Lawrence — whose irritable, affectionate essay remains the best criticism of Whitman — he does not say, "Look what I've been clever enough to observe!" but, "Feel as I feel! Think as I think!"

2.

I called it a familiar doubleness. He was not what he once proclaimed, "one of the roughs." As he wrote elsewhere, "I am not what you supposed but far different." When he read a poem on a rare occasion in public, apparently he spoke so softly as to be inaudible to all but the first row of his listeners. The others could hear nothing, and their response was understandably meager. But if you read a particular newspaper account, you would learn that Whitman had filled the auditorium with his booming, masculine voice, and that his recitation had been interrupted continually by applause. Whitman himself wrote and planted this news item.

Let me dwell on this anecdote. Many a man has exaggerated his accomplishments, some men even in writing of themselves in the third person. But the disparity between Whitman's performance when he spoke, and the performance he described as a reviewer, is almost beyond the credible. The man did not live in the world he saw, but in the Invisible World. With a lesser man, this might be a polite way of calling him a phoney, but the author of "Out of the Cradle Endlessly Rocking" is not to be dismissed, however many lies he may tell. Whitman's self-review only supports the ubiquity of his unworldliness. He may *think* he is merely puffing his fame, but really he testifies again to the pervasiveness of the dreamed self.

Whitman was born in Long Island on May 31, 1819. Four years later the family moved to Brooklyn, which was where he spent much of his life. He attended school for five years only, leaving at the age of eleven to go to work. Later he taught in country schools for a few years, but as a young man mostly made his living editing contentious newspapers. He wrote a few sentimental tracts and even a temperance novel, in which there is little evidence of talent. During these years he was reading widely and educating himself. He read British periodicals like the *Edinburgh Review*, and scientific books, and followed one deep interest after another. In the early 1850's, he worked as a carpenter, at the same time as he was writing the first edition of *Leaves of Grass*, which he published in 1855. At the end of his twenties or the beginning of his thirties, an extraordinary spiritual change turned the writer of political invective, who seemed committed to the world of action as a journalist, into the author of "Song of Myself."

Leaves of Grass was poorly received when it was received at all, except for the generous praise of Emerson, which

Whitman was quick to circulate and exploit. But Whitman persevered, revising and adding new poems, and publishing numerous editions until his death in 1892. During the Civil War and immediately thereafter he held government jobs in Washington, and suffered some persecution on account of the alleged obscenity of his work. It was around Washington that he acted as a male nurse to wounded soldiers, a period of his life which led to the poems of *Drum Taps.* He endured his first stroke early in life, and for many years lived a semi-invalid tranquility, enjoying his friendships, writing new poems and revising old ones. Though *Leaves of Grass* was largely ignored and occasionally attacked, it also attracted warm admirers and even disciples. Whitman never won general acceptance in America — as lesser poets like Longfellow and Whittier did — but he won the adulation of particular admirers, which was probably more important to him.

Maybe one of the reasons Whitman was able to turn himself from a journalist into a great poet was that a great poet was widely required, for patriotic purposes. The intellectual-nationalist "Young America" movement, which started in 1837, called for "a great Poet of the people," and a "Homer of the masses." Such requirements were the natural outcome of a successful democratic revolution, only fifty years old. (Whatever else it accomplished, the American revolution was a necessary prerequisite to an American literature.) Doubtless many young men phrased sentiments like these, which I take from a novel published in 1849. "We want a national literature commensurate with our mountains and rivers . . . a national epic that shall correspond to the size of the country . . . a national drama in which scope shall be given to our gigantic ideas and to the unparalleled activity of our people . . . In a word, we want a national literature altogether shaggy and unshorn, that shall shake the earth, like a herd of buffaloes thundering over the prairies." But the young man who wrote these lines was Henry Wadsworth Longfellow, whose contribution to our continental epic was *Hiawatha*. The Young America movement may have helped Whitman, as his feelings of patriotism did, and his assumed identity as a democratic spokesman. But his nationalism is ghostly. He spiritualizes the Mississippi and the Rockies as much as he later spiritualized "Passage to India" through "the seas of God."

In Whitman the familiar doubleness is not the Yeatsian self and anti-self. Even the two poetry-reading Whitmans — the real one and the one in the newspaper puff — are not opposites; one is a fantasy version of the other. The seen American and the spiritualized America are the ouside and the inside of the same idea.

It is interesting to speculate on the sources of this tendency to daydream an Invisible World. To suggest motives is not to reduce the work of art to the motive, though literary people in their terror of psychoanalysis often think so. (To speak of Dostoevsky's unconscious urge to parricide is not to make *Crime and Punishment* a crime.) Whitman's erotic feeling, as it shows itself in his poems, is almost entirely homosexual. It does not matter whether Whitman made love with men or not; but there is no ignoring that his erotic imagery is phallic. Some passages from "Song of Myself" and "The Sleepers," which I will quote a little later, can serve as examples of this imagery. As with all other parts of the world he saw, Whitman spiritualized his homosexual feelings and turned them into visions of brotherhood and of self-love.

Possibly his tendency toward reverie arose from the fact that actions he most desired were self-prohibited.

3.

A history of American poetry could be written as a series of reactions to Walt Whitman. Ezra Pound in *Lustra* (1916) made "A Pact":

I make a pact with you, Walt Whitman—
I have detested you long enough.
I come to you as a grown child
Who has had a pig-headed father;
I am old enough now to make friends.
It was you that broke the new wood,
Now is a time for carving.
We have one sap and one root—
Let there be commerce between us.

Pound's good-natured arrogance does not conceal his respect. In a prose essay in 1909 Pound said, "I honor him for he prophesied me," and called him, "my spiritual father." Yet his attitude in an earlier essay was frequently embarrassed. "Mentally I am a Walt Whitman who has learned to wear a collar and a dress shirt."

Most American poets have been mandarins of one sort or another, and Whitman embarrasses them socially, like a cousin who turns up at one's dinner party wearing a tie with a large palm tree painted on it. Whitman doesn't know how to behave. He uses foreign phrases incorrectly because he is both ignorant and pretentious. He is a half-

learned encyclopedia, and the unlearned half is continually exposed. Well-bred types must look the other way.
Some enjoy being ironical, like Oliver Wendell Holmes
who observed that Whitman included in his "hospitable
vocabulary words which no English dictionary recognizes
as belonging to the language — words which will be looked for in vain outside of his own pages." As is well-
known in Europe, there is nothing *quite* so cultured as a
cultured American. Henry James knew it, and kept right
on being it. Feeling cultureless, we have decided to take all
culture upon ourselves. Most American writers have been
middle-class and well-educated. The critical habit of
dividing American writers into palefaces and redskins is
deceptive: though there is a tolerable difference between
Bret Harte and James Russell Lowell, the redskin is usually only a paleface with pancake make-up. The Beat
generation was largely bright Columbia boys who took
over the reservation of North Beach, scalped the
aborigines, and passed for red. The redskin American
writer resembles Teddy Roosevelt, the effete Easterner
who goes west to toughen up and become a man: he turns
into a rough rider, "one of the roughs." Since the success
of Gregory Corso, the woods have become full of
professors in loincloths, trying desperately to talk with
acceptably incorrect grammar. Put an academic poet on a
platform with Charles Bukowski and he starts saying
fuck.

Though Whitman's affectation of roughness resembles
the Teddy Roosevelt syndrome, it is entirely different; he
did not come from Oyster Bay; he did not go to Harvard.
He is, in effect, a peasant poet like Whittier. We have no
others. William Carlos Williams wrote poems out of
working class life, but critics go out of their way to call

attention to his professional status as a physician. Since all American poets have been members of (or disaffiliates from) the educated middle-class, Whitman has been a social embarrassment or a social weapon. Palefaces have feared him because he represented an alien world, and redskins have used him against the bourgeoisie, which is their parents. If you are putting down Henry James, or Harvard College, it may be useful to admire something in Whitman which has no virtue except its antipathy to those institutions. Few were able to make a genuine pact with him. Praised or blamed for social reasons (the academics of "American Studies" — the relative redskins of the classroom — *needed* a great poet, even if they couldn't tell one from a third baseman), Whitman has been praised and blamed with almost equal irrelevance. Readers who grew up on the new criticism found no way of dealing with his poems at all. "Have you felt so proud to get at the meaning of poems?" Whitman asks in "Song of Myself." Well, yes, and Whitman's poems do not have that kind of meaning.

Now, I think, Americans are no longer so afraid of being oafs in the drawing room; we can stop being careful or defiant; we can forget Whitman's mispronunciations. We can read him as Lawrence did, with occasional anger and with love:

Whitman, the great poet, has meant so much to me. Whitman, the one man making a way ahead. Whitman, the one pioneer. And only Whitman . . . In Europe the would-be pioneers are mere innovators . . . Ahead of all poets, pioneering into the wilderness of unopened life, Whitman . . . His wide, strange camp at the end of the great high-road.

Lawrence takes over Whitman's metaphor of the pioneers, and neither of them is talking about Daniel Boone. ". . . the wilderness of unopened life" is their subject, the unexplored and inward continent of the spirit, each man's internal America. My own ability to read Whitman, after years of finding innumerable ways to resist him, was aided by a contemporary poet, Louis Simpson, when he wrote "Walt Whitman at Bear Mountain":

Neither on horseback nor seated,
But like himself, squarely on two feet,
The poet of death and lilacs
Loafs by the footpath. Even the bronze looks alive
Where it is folded like cloth. And he seems friendly.

"Where is the Mississippi panorama
And the girl who played the piano?
Where are you, Walt?
The Open Road goes to the used-car lot.

"Where is the nation you promised?
These houses built of wood sustain
Colossal snows,
And the light above the street is sick to death.

"As for the people — see how they neglect you!
Only a poet pauses to read the inscription."

"I am here," he answered.
"It seems you have found me out.
Yet, did I not warn you that it was Myself
I advertised? Were my words not sufficiently plain?

"I gave no prescriptions,
And those who have taken my moods for prophecies
Mistake the matter."
Then, vastly amused, — "Why do you reproach me?
I freely confess I am wholly disreputable.
Yet I am happy, because you have found me out."

A crocodile in wrinkled metal loafing . . . .

Then all the realtors,
Pickpockets, salesmen, and the actors performing
Official scenarios,
Turned a deaf ear, for they had contracted
American dreams.

But the man who keeps a store on a lonely road,
And the housewife who knows she's dumb,
And the earth, are relieved.

All that grave weight of America
Cancelled! Like Greece and Rome.
The future in ruins!
The castles, the prisons, the cathedrals
Unbuilding, and roses
Blossoming from the stones that are not there . . .

The clouds are lifting from the high Sierras,
The Bay mists clearing;
And the angel in the gate, the flowering plum,
Dances like Italy, imagining red.

Only when the castles, prisons and cathedrals are unbuilt can the world of the spirit, which is found in Myself, dance like Italy.

4.

Whitman nods, like everyone else, mostly in moments of rhetoric or bombast. But there is no point in dwelling on these flaws in a huge construction, except when the flaws have been singled out for praise. The schoolteachers in their search for a genteel Whitman have singled out the ghastly lyric "O Captain My Captain." If they have read the great poem out of Lincoln's death, "When Lilacs Last in the Dooryard Bloom'd," they have tried to make it a poem in praise of President Lincoln — another outwardness — rather than a poem of universal mourning:

> *(Nor for you, for one alone,*
> *Blossoms and branches green to coffins all I bring,*
> *For fresh as the morning, thus would I chant a song for*
>   *you O sane and sacred death.*
>
> *All over bouquets of roses,*
> *O death, I cover you over with roses and early lilies,*
> *But mostly and now the lilac that blooms the first,*
> *Copious I break, I break the sprigs from the bushes,*
> *With loaded arms I come, pouring for you,*
> *For you and the coffins all of you O death.)*

He writes of death as a lover; he mourns the loss of the impossibility of the love he desires, which is like the satisfaction of the baby at the breast — the loss for which everyone mourns, and which unites love and death in all of us. Love and death come together in another great long poem, "Out of the Cradle Endlessly Rocking"; "my brother," here, is a male bird that has lost its mate:

Yes my brother I know,
The rest might not, but I have treasur'd every note,
For more than once dimly down to the beach gliding,
Silent, avoiding the moonbeams, blending myself with
    the shadows,

Recalling now the obscure shapes, the echoes, the
    sounds and sights after their sorts,
The white arms out in the breakers tirelessly tossing,
I, with bare feet, a child, the wind wafting my hair,
Listen'd long and long.

Listen'd to keep, to sing, now translating the notes,
Following you my brother.

Soothe! soothe! soothe!
Close on its wave soothes the wave behind,
And again another behind embracing and lapping,
    every one close,
But my love soothes not me, not me.

Low hangs the moon, it rose late,
It is lagging — O I think it is heavy with love, with love.

O madly the sea pushes upon the land,
With love, with love.

O night! do I not see my love fluttering out among the
    breakers?
What is that little black thing I see there in the white?

The poet of mourning is also the poet of internal exploration, and of the self-love which must exist before love can exist. "Song of Myself," from the beginning of his life as a poet, is central to his work. Here he sets out what he must do. His variety is prodigious, and everything has its own excellence and grace. Here is a section:

The big doors of the country barn stand open and
   ready,
The dried grass of the harvest-time loads the slow-
   drawn wagon,
The clear light plays on the brown, gray and green in-
   termingled,
The armfuls are pack'd to the sagging mow.

I am there, I help, I came stretch'd atop of the load,
I felt its soft jolts, one leg reclined on the other,
I jump from the cross-beams and seize the clover and
   timothy,
And roll head over heels and tangle my hair full of
   wisps.

And here are some lines from a later section, so different:

Walt Whitman, a kosmos, of Manhattan the son,
Turbulent, fleshy, sensual, eating, drinking and
   breeding,
No sentimentalist, no stander above men and women or
   apart from them,
No more modest than immodest.

Unscrew the locks from the doors!
Unscrew the doors themselves from their jambs!

Whoever degrades another degrades me,
And whatever is done or said returns at last to me.

Through me the afflatus surging and surging . . . .

* * * * * * * *

If I worship one thing more than another it shall be the
    spread of my own body, or any part of it.
Translucent mould of me it shall be you!
Shaded ledges and rests it shall be you!
Firm masculine colter it shall be you!
Whatever goes to the tilth of me it shall be you!
You my rich blood! your milky stream pale strippings
    of my life!
Breast that presses against other breasts it shall be you!
My brain it shall be your occult convolutions!
Root of wash'd sweet-flag! timorous pond-snipe! nest
    of guarded duplicate eggs! it shall be you!
Mixed tussled hay of head, beard, brawn, it shall be
    you!
Trickling sap of maple, fibre of manly wheat, it shall be
    you!
Sun so generous it shall be you!
Vapors lighting and shading my face it shall be you!
You sweaty brooks and dews it shall be you!
Winds whose soft-tickling genitals rub against me it
    shall be you!

Broad muscular fields, branches of live oak, loving
    lounger in my winding paths, it shall be you!
Hands I have taken, face I have kiss'd, mortal I have
    ever touch'd, it shall be you!

145

I dote on myself, there is a lot of me and all so
    luscious . . . .

"Song of Myself" will not allow itself to be overlooked,
but another great early poem has remained largely
obscure. I mean "The Sleepers," an exploration of dream
images that remind me of Henry Moore's Reclining
Figures, or even more of the drawings Moore made of men
and women sleeping underground during the air raids of
London. In late editions of *Leaves of Grass*, Whitman
buried the poem deep in the volume, and omitted some of
the more surreal and erotic passages, like this one:

O hotcheek'd and blushing! O foolish hectic!
O for pity's sake, no one must see me now! . . . my
    clothes were stolen while I was abed,
Now I am thrust forth, where shall I run?

Pier that I saw dimly last night, when I look'd from the
    windows,
Pier out from the main, let me catch myself with you,
    and stay . . . I will not chafe you;
I feel ashamed to go naked about the world.
I am curious to know where my feet stand. . . . and
    what this is flooding me, childhood or man-
    hood . . . and the hunger that crosses the bridge
    between.

The cloth laps a first sweet eating and drinking,
Laps life-swelling yolks. . . . laps ear of rose-corn,
    milky and just-ripen'd;
The white teeth stay, and the boss-tooth advances in
    darkness,

And liquor is spill'd on lips and bosoms by touching
glasses and the best liquor afterward.

The poem as a whole is not so particularly sexual; its
openness and its irrational sequence are astonishingly
modern.

Subject matter associates two groups of poems, the
"Calamus" poems of "manly love" (the calamus has a
phallic spear), and the poems of the Civil War, originally
collected as *Drum Taps*. Typical of the greatness of these
poems is "Vigil Strange I Kept on the Field One Night,"
which ends:

...my son in his grave, in his rude-dug grave I de-
posited,
Ending my vigil strange with that, vigil of night and
battle-field dim,
Vigil for boy of responding kisses, (never again on
earth responding,)
Vigil for comrade swiftly slain, vigil I never forget, how
as day brighten'd,
I rose from the child ground and folded my soldier well
in his blanket,
And buried him where he fell.

Though the long poems are Whitman's most celebrated,
he can be a master as well of the short intense image. Take
a poem like "A Farm Picture":

Through the ample open door of the peaceful country
barn,
A sunlit pasture field with cattle and horses feeding,
And haze and vista, and the far horizon fading away.

This poem is more imagist than anything in *Des Imagistes*, and creates an emblem of pure being, the floating reverie which occurs in the longer poems. Or take a Lawrentian poem, written in 1880, "The Dalliance of the Eagles":

> Skirting the river road, (my forenoon walk, my rest,)
> Skyward in air a sudden muffled sound, the dalliance of the eagles,
> The rushing amorous contact high in space together,
> The clinching interlocking claws, a living, fierce, gyrating wheel,
> Four beating wings, two beaks, a swirling mass tight grappling.
> In tumbling turning clustering loops, straight downward falling,
> Till o'er the river pois'd, the twain yet one, a moment's lull,
> A motionless still balance in the air, then parting, talons loosing,
> Upward again on slow-firm pinions slanting, their separate diverse flight,
> She hers, he his, pursuing.

This poem is more violent than Whitman usually wishes to be, and illustrates among other things that he can do almost anything.

It is interesting to compare *Leaves of Grass* and the *Cantos* — both world-books, and not books but men; but in the *Cantos* information is structural, and in *Leaves* it is illustrative, a totem always of inwardness. When Whitman wants to praise a new invention linking all men, he speaks of "The seas inlaid with eloquent gentle wires."

The gentleness has nothing to do with a cable under the Atlantic, everything to do with a spirit that transforms the world seen. As Leslie Fiedler says, "His mode is reverie; his voice is that of one talking to himself as he falls asleep in the haze of lazy noonday or at the onset of night. What binds Whitman's poems together is not the logic of persuasion or pictorial form, but what we have come to label a little misleadingly 'stream of consciousness': the secret order of repressed wishes and fears that links impression to impression..." A poetry of wishes and fears — ultimately a poetry of the deep mind that all men share.

Pound said, "We have one sap and one root." He was speaking of place and of the vulgar tongue, and he is right enough, but one could wish for the greatness of Pound that some of the reverie of Whitman could have been added to it. We are all Whitman if we can let ourselves be, if the sap and the root are allowed to grow and are not pruned by American outwardness. (Pound's image has the wood carved by technique; American poets have tended to evade greatness by concentrating on technique instead of on spirit.) Whitman is the poet of the America that Jose Marti (who heard him lecture in 1887) could see, behind the America of prisons and cathedrals. He is the poet of the America that Pablo Neruda loves; Neruda and Whitman have much in common — poets who are both nationalist and surrealist, poets of wishes and fears, poets of love and inwardness, and the two greatest poets of the hemisphere.

The Poet And The Battle (1965)*

I N September, 1958, I was reading Douglas and Dunbar, which made me think about the battle of Flodden. Something struck me, and I found myself writing about the battle without knowing what I was going to say about it. It was a little poem of three six-line stanzas, written in a short unmetrical line which usually had two speech stresses. I worked at the poem for a month or two, improving lines here and there, but I never found the real motive to it. The first stanza was good writing, I thought, but the whole poem simply didn't matter. Finally I became impatient, and put it away in a drawer.

The next January I read in a newspaper that Edwin Muir was dead. I was unhappy, for I had become fond of Edwin and Willa during their year in this country. I felt close to him, and was looking forward to seeing him a year later in England. That night I drifted into the vague, dreamy condition which often precedes a poem — the first draft of a poem, I should say, since for me it is always necessary to revise in the clear mornings the gifts of the dreamy night. I began three poems then. One of them was about Edwin's death. Although I had forgotten the Flodden poem, the poem about Edwin was the same number of the same sort of lines in the same number of stanzas.

Then it began to act like the Flodden poem, too. It had one stanza which was better than the others. Although the poem as a whole had the obvious point of grief, I realized that it lacked imaginative wholeness. I struggled with it for a month or more, until the morning when I remembered that the Flodden poem was written in precisely the same form. I decided to compare the two, and I found the old poem, and I recognized that the two poems were really one.

The first stanza of the Flodden poem became the first stanza of "O Flodden Field." The first stanza of the poem about Edwin became the second. Elements of both poems, and new lines which united the themes, made the last stanza. It took me a month or two to *finish* the poem, for a few words were difficult to find. But the essential act in the writing of "O Flodden Field" was the confrontation of the two false starts.

O Flodden Field

in memory of Edwin Muir

The learned King fought
Like a fool, flanked
and outtricked, who hacked
in a corner of cousins
until the ten thousand
swords lay broken,
and the women walked
in their houses alone.

On a journey among horses,
the spirit of a man who died
only a week ago
is walking through heather
and forgets that its body
had seventy years.
Wild horses are singing,
and voices of the rocks.

The spirit from the bone-yard
finds a new life, in the field
where the King's wound
built the blackness of Glasgow
and the smoke of the air.
The spirit, like a boy,
picks up from the heather
a whole sword.

A friend who is a psychologist believes that when I wrote the original Flodden poem, I was worrying about Edwin. I tend to agree. The battle of Flodden was the death of Scotland. I thought of Edwin as a Scot, though he came from the Orkneys. I had been much impressed to read, in his *Autobiography*, of his family's suffering in the slums of Glasgow; in the original Flodden poem I referred to these slums. Finally, I knew that he was ill, and was selfishly worried that he would not live until we got to England. The process of a poem is like an iceberg; the bulk of it lives in a dark place, hidden from the conscious eye. Only the luck of the imagination allows us to report the great weight under the water.

Waking Up The Giant (1969)*

W HEN A poet writes a poem, I believe that much of his intention is hidden — and hidden from himself. A poem is not a mechanically realized object of a conscious purpose. At least, there are large portions of poems which exist outside intentions, the way saying one thing in conversation we may communicate something else — perhaps the opposite, perhaps a reservation — by facial expression or gesture.

If everyone understood the undirected nature of composition, it would dispel a false but prevalent idea. This idea is the sense that there is a real, single "meaning" to a poem, which it is our object in reading to discover. If you ask someone to define what this "meaning" is, chances are he will tell you some variation on a phrase like "What the poet was trying to say," or "what he had in mind before he wrote the poem," or simply "the poet's intention."

---

*Adapted from *The Pleasures of Poetry*, Harper & Row, 1971.

This idea is psychologically naive. If someone interprets his own dream for us, we do not necessarily believe him. It may occur to us that he might have good reasons for misinterpreting his own dream. A poet is usually aware that he is not in total control of his poem — not in total *conscious* control, that is; some less lighted part of his mind may be controlling the poem firmly. Many poets nowadays — after general acceptance of the idea of the unconscious mind — feel that the dark parts of their mind write the best poetry, and so they try to do away with light, by automatic writing and other methods of suppressing rational thought, including drugs.

But even poets who are dedicated to presenting a reasonable surface realize that other things are happening inside their poems. Even after he had written his "Four Quartets," with all their religious content, T.S. Eliot said that in poetry all content was only ostensible content; that if the poem had a real life, probably something was going on of which the poet was unaware. So the idea of conscious intentions, as creating "the meaning" of a poem, is merely silly. All we *know* is the words on the page. If the poet himself swore out an affidavit, the same day he wrote the poem, and headed the affidavit: THIS IS WHAT I WAS TRYING TO SAY, I would immediately disbelieve him: "Who is *he* to tell *me*? He must be trying to cover something up. I will take a closer look at his poem."

The reasons for the secret life in poems do not lie in the art of poetry but in human life. We are all complicated and our feelings are many sided — so many sided that we cannot identify, or know consciously, all sides. The same ambiguity that inhabits an honest poem (a dishonest poem is frequently one which a frightened poet has overcontrolled into single-mindedness) inhabits our daily lives, and shows up in our dreams, our verbal slips, our changes of mind and heart, and our sense that our lives are not clear and singly directed, but a shifting combination of opposing forces. No one is *wholly* aware of the motives behind any serious action. No more is a poet wholly aware of what makes him go.

To illustrate this point, I want to use my own experience. When I was twenty-five or twenty-six, I wrote a poem called "The Sleeping Giant," which is the name of a hill in Hamden, Connecticut, where I grew up. From certain angles the hill does look like a sleeping giant — head, neck, chest, waist, the legs trailing off. When I was a boy I climbed a trail to the top of it, and I broiled hot dogs at a picnic place near the bottom. When I was beginning to publish as a poet, I happened to think of the Sleeping Giant, and either remembered or invented the thought that a small child, hearing his father say, "There's the Sleeping Giant," might believe that the hill was a real sleeping giant, and be frightened.

At that time in my life as a poet, I needed to feel wholly in control of a poem. I knew before I started writing where I was going to go in the poem. (In retrospect, it now seems to me that the better poems of that period always went places I didn't know they were going. The ones that did what I told them to, like obedient children, are deplorable.) I decided to write a poem about a child being frightened of the Sleeping Giant, and then getting older — going to school perhaps — and realizing that the giant was not real. It was to be a poem about illusion and reality.

It took me a long time to write it. First, I tried doing it in four-line stanzas of blank verse. I made the story come out right, but the poem did not feel right to me. It lacked the click of the box. I decided that, for some reason I could not understand, it was the *sort* of poem that had to be rhymed. I took it apart and rhymed the second and fourth lines of each stanza. It began to sound better. After maybe six or eight months of intermittent work, the poem was in good shape, I thought — except for the last line. It would not come right. I needed an image which would allow a time span during which the illusion could be dispelled, an image which would kill the giant, and which would be an outdoor scene and thus continue the metaphorical area of the poem, and which would belong to the child's world — all at once. Then one morning (I got up at six and worked on my poems from about six to eight in the morning), I was copying the poem out and I watched — with amazement and gratitude — while my right hand, all by itself with no apparent help from my brain, wrote the line that I wanted. Here is the poem that I finished that day:

The whole day long, under the walking sun
That poised an eye on me from its high floor,
Holding my toy beside the clapboard house
I looked for him, the summer I was four.

I was afraid the waking arm would break
From the loose earth and rub against his eyes
A fist of trees, and the whole country tremble
In the exultant labor of his rise;

Then he with giant steps in the small streets
Would stagger, cutting off the sky, to seize
The roofs from house and home because we had
Covered his shape with dirt and planted trees;

And then kneel down and rip with fingernails

A trench to pour the enemy Atlantic
Into our basin, and the water rush,
With the streets full and all the voices frantic.

That was the summer I expected him.
Later the high and watchful sun instead
Walked low behind the house, and school began,
And winter pulled a sheet over his head.

As it turned out, my hand wrote the whole poem, without the help of my brain, because it was not a "little thing about illusion and reality" as I thought it was. But it was years before I discovered the real content of the poem.

At first, I was pleased with what I had written, in a small way, and I sent the poem to the *New Yorker*, which printed it, and I put it in my first book, and then people began to praise it and editors to anthologize it. I began to be offended for my other, more serious (as I thought) poems. I began to dislike "The Sleeping Giant" as one might resent the one child whom one's friends preferred to one's other children. I could not see what people saw in it.

Five years later I read an article which a poet put together about my poems. He pointed out that I had written many times about the relationship between fathers and sons; but the best of these poems, he said, was "The Sleeping Giant." I felt the chills on my spine one feels when something hits home; I suddenly saw (and was able to see partly because my attitude toward poetry and the human mind was changing; I was more able to accept the unconscious and uncontrolled contents of poetry) that my fear of the giant was a dream-representation of the baby's fear of grown-ups. Every culture contains myths of giants, as if giants once did inhabit the earth; and indeed they did and do; when you are two feet long the creatures who stand over your crib are giants, and something inside you remembers them until you die.

I looked at the poem more closely, and saw that it was classically Oedipal; the boy in the poem was afraid of the giant "... because we had/Covered his shape with dirt ..." The boy assumed that "we" had buried the giant; the fear of killing and the fear of being killed are simultaneous feelings in the psyche, the two sides of the Oedipal terror. Without knowing what I was doing, I had rehearsed an ancient story; the primitive engine made the poem go, for me, and — I am sure without most of them knowing it — my readers too.

It is rare, in my experience, that a critic points out an unconscious content which a poet can accept. Often the poet does not want to admit to himself feelings of which he might be ashamed. At the time I wrote "The Sleeping Giant," I would not have admitted the feelings that made the poem. What is more, if I had been aware of them, I could not have written them down. So my blindness was helpful to me. Now — when in writing a poem I *know* I don't know what I am revealing or discovering — my poems are often fantastic or nonsensical on the surface. I no longer need, or even want, an ostensible content, a neat little argument, or a story about "illusion and reality." But frequently when I have finished a poem I see the inner content — or I think I do, or I see part of it. That is how I can tell I have finished a poem.

Still, I have had the experience of only finding out "what I was trying to say" after publishing the poem — sometimes by hearing myself talk about it at a poetry reading, or sometimes with a little help from my friends. It is the hidden content which makes a poem *go*, for writer and reader alike. It is powerful stuff, or we wouldn't have had to hide it in the first place. The images of the poem release the giant from his long sleep.

The Expression Without The Song (1969)*

F OR a long time I have been looking for a way to describe a kind of poetry. This poetry is inward, dreamlike and fantastic; it is not precisely surreal, it resembles Spanish poets more than it resembles French surrealists. It is able to be tender, it is often amusing, and it can be deeply moving. I have called it "expressionist" because it distorts reality to show feeling, but I think the reference to a school of painting confuses things. I have used a phrase that William Empson made up, "poems without legs"; he meant by legs such traditional structures as narrative or logic. (Empson used the phrase contemptuously, but that doesn't matter; when the critic called the painters "wild beasts" he wasn't intending to compliment them.) But Empson's phrase pictures the poem as double amputee. The poems I call legless gain something by forswearing traditional organization.

Then recently a friend showed me a passage from Wittgenstein. In the fourth of his *Lectures on Aesthetics*, Wittgenstein says, "A man may sing with expression and without expression. Then why not leave out the song —

160

could you hear the expression then?" I love the notion. The question is intended to expose nonsense, but I want to brush aside the logic and take the phrase for my own purposes. This poetry gives the expression without the song.

The song is the old baggage of ostensible content which, as Eliot says, is never the true content. "The leaves fall in the autumn and come back in the spring," etc. "I am historically determined to lack Christian faith, alas," etc. Who needs this junk? If poetry were judged by what usually passes for content, the best of it would be eighth-rate philosophy, on the intellectual level of textbooks and the *Reader's Digest.* If you love old poems, you have always loved the expression and not the song, though your brain may have concentrated on the song. You have loved the shapeliness of the words in your mouth, and you have loved the inward speech of the second language of poetry — the private voice underneath the public speech, that the poet himself is aware of only dimly.

There is another kind of poetry, a poetry of the intelligence and without mystery. Auden is a contemporary example, especially in his later poetry which resembles the conversation of an intelligent man. Occasionally the second language comes through, but mostly we have the *pages de journal* of a literate intellectual, and not the poetry of expressiveness. For me, it is a lesser kind of poetry. When I read essays, I would just as soon they came in paragraphs. Poetry is written in lines because lines are a way of controlling what happens in the mouth. Poetry happens in the mouth, and by the mouth to the imagination, and the dream country of wishes and fears. Ideas happen in the eye, and from the eye to the top of the mind, the place of reason, civilization, charm, wit, and governments.

But song and expression need not be enemies; they can exist together. Most great poetry has used the hook of a song (reflections and stories and arguments) to hang its expression on, just as old painting used verisimilitude (to landscape and figure) as a vehicle for its expressions of feeling in color, shape and texture. When you liberate the poem from the obligation to have an ostensible meaning, strange things happen. Images set free from realistic narrative or from logic grow out of each other by association, and poems move by an inward track of feeling. Perhaps the song in some sense is still there, but it does not leave you humming the tune.

Here is a great poem that has a song and that has expression, too, Thomas Hardy's "During Wind and Rain."

They sing their dearest songs —
He, she, all of them — yea,
Trebel and tenor and bass,
*   And one to play;*
With the candles mooning each face . . .
*   Ah, no; the years O!*
How the sick leaves reel down in throngs!

They clear the creeping moss —
Elders and juniors — aye,
Making the pathway neat
*   And the garden gay;*
And they build a shady seat . . .
*   Ah, no; the years, the years;*
See, the white storm-birds wing across!

They are blithely breakfasting all —
Men and maidens — yea,

Under the summer tree,
  With a glimpse of the bay,
While pet fowl come to the knee . . .
  Ah, no; the years O!
And the rotten rose is ript from the wall.

They change to a high new house,
He, she, all of them — aye,
Clocks and carpets and chairs
  On the lawn all day,
And brightest things that are theirs . . .
  Ah, no; the years, the years;
Down their carved names the rain-drop ploughs

The ostensible content is simple: "Families have a lot of pleasure together, but then people grow old and die. Times four." Yet read the poem intimately, and the paraphrase is ridiculously trivial. The paraphrase is conventional melancholy and the expression of the poem is joyous. There is talk going on in a language which the top of our mind does not understand, but which reaches through our mouths the country of wishes and fears. At the center of the poem is the mystery. Hardy's poem is obscure, like all good poems: our minds cannot name the causes of our response to it.

In the poem that leaves out the song and concentrates on expression, the obscurity is more candid. Remember the little poem by Wallace Stevens, "Disillusionment of Ten O'Clock." It is one of the few poems written by an American, until the last few years, which is mostly expression.

Disillusionment of Ten O'Clock

The houses are haunted
By white night-gowns.
None are green,
Or purple with green rings,
Or green with yellow rings,
Or yellow with blue rings.
None of them are strange,
With socks of lace
And beaded ceintures.
People are not going
To dream of baboons and periwinkles.
Only, here and there, an old sailor,
Drunk and asleep in his boots,
Catches tigers
In red weather.

The paraphrase here is as banal as the paraphrase of Hardy's poem: "Folks around here don't have any imagination," or "These proper people are unimaginative; improper people have a more exciting inner life." However you paraphrase it, you are not going to cope with a sailor who catches tigers in red weather. This poem is obscure, like Hardy's, in that the words move and delight us in our irrational selves. The poem lives in the country of dream, asleep in its boots.

For most of the years since Stevens wrote "Disillusionment of Ten O'Clock" (it was published more than fifty years ago), American poets have written poems the old way, with ostensible contents fully visible. Sometimes they have written very well; Robert Frost is moving and mysterious, and always keeps up a surface. But in the last decade, as part of a general opening-up of the imagination in poetry, young poets have increasingly sought to discover and express their irrational selves. They have not followed any rigid program — the rule book hurt French surrealism — though they have learned from modern European and Latin American poetry in general.

One of the methods of this new poetry is to suppress old progressive forms like narrative or argument. The precise reverse — anti-narrative is a story that makes no sense; illogic is useful if it is gross enough — can suppress trite associations, but of course takes some of its shapeliness from the order it is mocking. (An old example is "Jabberwocky.") There is also a poetry — more like the Wallace Stevens poem — in which the progress is fantastic, in which expression sings loud and clear, without a song. Here is a famous example, translated from the German by Christopher Middleton, Paul Celan's "Fugue of Death":

Black milk of daybreak we drink it at nightfall
we drink it at noon in the morning we drink it at night
drink it and drink it
we are digging a grave in the sky it is ample to lie there
A man in the house he plays with the serpents he writes
he writes when the night falls to Germany your golden
      hair Margarete
he writes it and walks from the house the stars glitter he
      whistles his dogs up
he whistles his Jews out and orders a grave to be dug in
      the earth
he commands us now on with the dance

Black milk of daybreak we drink you at night

*we drink in the mornings at noon we drink you at
   nightfall*
drink you and drink you
A man in the house he plays with the serpents he writes
*he writes when the night falls to Germany your golden
   hair Margarete*
*Your ashen hair Shulamith we are digging a grave in
   the sky it is ample to lie there*
*He shouts stab deeper in the earth you there you others
   you sing and you play*
*he grabs at the iron in his belt and swings it and blue are
   his eyes*
*stab deeper your spades you there and you others play
   on for the dancing*

Black milk of daybreak we drink you at night
*we drink you at noon in the mornings we drink you at
   nightfall*
drink you and drink you
a man in the house your golden hair Margarete
your ashen hair Shulamith he plays with the serpents

*He shouts play sweeter death's music death comes as a
   master from Germany*
*he shouts stroke darker the strings and as smoke you
   shall climb to the sky*
*then you'll have a grave in the clouds it is ample to lie
   there*

Black milk of daybreak we drink you at night
*we drink you at noon death comes as a master from
   Germany*
*we drink you at nightfall and morning we drink you
   and drink you*

THE EXPRESSION WITHOUT THE SONG

a master from Germany death comes with eyes that are
*   blue*
with a bullet of lead he will hit in the mark he will hit
*   you*
a man in the house your golden hair Margarete
he hunts us down with his dogs in the sky he gives us a
*   grave*
he plays with the serpents and dreams death comes as a
*   master from Germany*
your golden hair Margarete
your ashen hair Shulamith

The poem's eloquence is great, its expressiveness and power; but it speaks in the second language, without an old surface, associating and inventing and amalgamating. Don't try humming it.